MATH

5

Practice 101 Minutes Weekly to Master Your Math Skills

PRACTICE WORKBOOK 2

- ✓ **Number Theory, LCM, GCF**
- ✓ **Fraction, Ratio and Percentage**
- ✓ **Time Related Problems, Measurements**
- ✓ **Probability and Possible Combinations**

101Minute.com

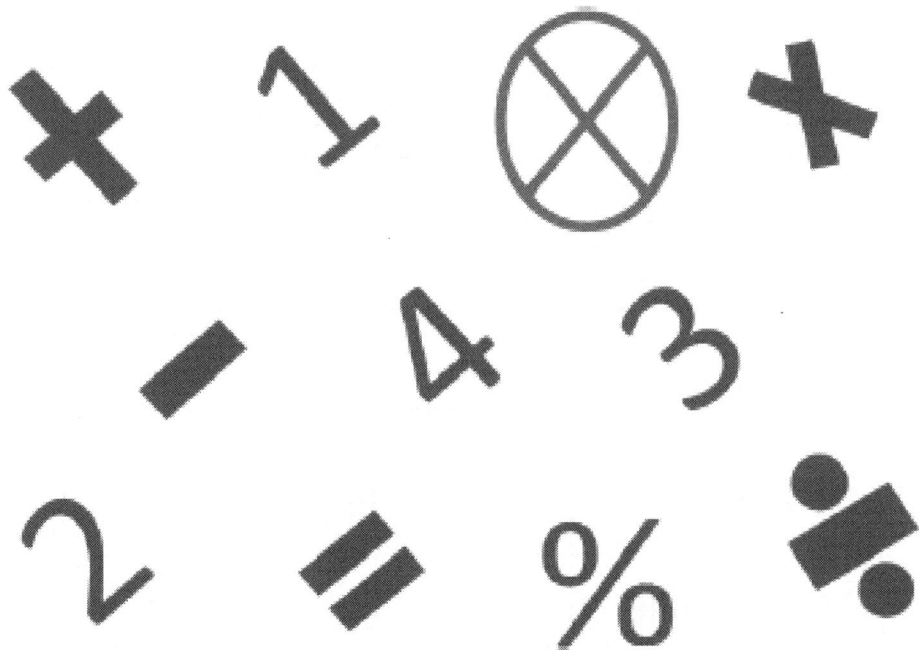

Ritesh Arora

About 101Minute.com

Welcome to 101Minute.com, a guide dedicated to help students excel academically.

We are focused on creating educational programs that help to enhance student's skills across various grades and subjects. Modules are designed per grade level that progressively enhances their skill and confidence each day.

Each subject category has several quizzes designed to assess student's mastery with the concept. By consistently devoting 101 minutes per week, students can demonstrate significant improvement.

We are committed to serving our student community by building effective tools and reward programs. We are open to receiving feedback on how we can improve to make this an even better experience for our students. Our goal is to create a fun and learning social educational environment for students, and reward them for their achievements.

Please visit us at 101Minute.com.

TABLE OF CONTENTS

1. DIVISIBLE PROBLEMS (TRUE OR FALSE)

Verify whether each of the following statement is correct (true) or not (false)?

1. Is 13869 divisible by 9?
   a) True
   b) False

2. Is 10878 divisible by 4?
   a) False
   b) True

3. Is 1831 divisible by 2?
   a) False
   b) True

4. Is 18821 divisible by 11?
   a) True
   b) False

5. Is 3471 divisible by 2?
   a) True
   b) False

6. Is 12381 divisible by 6?
   a) False
   b) True

7. Is 12816 divisible by 6?
   a) True
   b) False

8. Is 14505 divisible by 5?
   a) True
   b) False

9. Is 148 divisible by 11?
   a) True
   b) False

10. Is 6025 divisible by 9?
    a) False
    b) True

11. Is 1892 divisible by 2?
    a) True
    b) False

12. Is 7598 divisible by 4?
    a) False
    b) True

13. Is 3093 divisible by 3?
    a) True
    b) False

14. Is 23915 divisible by 10?
    a) False
    b) True

15. Is 8193 divisible by 3?
   a) True
   b) False

16. Is 1707 divisible by 5?
   a) False
   b) True

17. Is 20758 divisible by 7?
   a) False
   b) True

18. Is 543 divisible by 3?
   a) True
   b) False

19. Is 121 divisible by 11?
   a) True
   b) False

20. Is 5807 divisible by 5?
   a) False
   b) True

21. Is 192 divisible by 2?
   a) True
   b) False

22. Is 9278 divisible by 7?
   a) False
   b) True

23. Is 3538 divisible by 7?
   a) False
   b) True

24. Is 4318 divisible by 4?
   a) False
   b) True

25. Is 21497 divisible by 7?
   a) True
   b) False

26. Is 4464 divisible by 4?
   a) True
   b) False

27. Is 5452 divisible by 3?
   a) False
   b) True

28. Is 25248 divisible by 8?
   a) True
   b) False

29. Is 4700 divisible by 8?
   a) False
   b) True

30. Is 3647 divisible by 7?
   a) True
   b) False

31. Is 9907 divisible by 5?
   a) False
   b) True

32. Is 4848 divisible by 8?
   a) True
   b) False

33. Is 9597 divisible by 7?
   a) True
   b) False

34. Is 28171 divisible by 11?
   a) True
   b) False

35. Is 16260 divisible by 10?
   a) True
   b) False

36. Is 191 divisible by 2?
   a) True
   b) False

37. Is 1755 divisible by 5?
   a) True
   b) False

38. Is 3592 divisible by 2?
   a) True
   b) False

39. Is 2616 divisible by 6?
   a) True
   b) False

40. Is 7760 divisible by 10?
   a) True
   b) False

2. GREATEST COMMON FACTOR

1. What is the greatest common factor of 5 and 10?

2. What is the greatest common factor of 18 and 24?

3. What is the greatest common factor of 30 and 50?

4. What is the greatest common factor of 6 and 10?

5. What is the greatest common factor of 1 and 2?

6. What is the greatest common factor of 6 and 9?

7. What is the greatest common factor of 9 and 12?

8. What is the greatest common factor of 18 and 27?

9. What is the greatest common factor of 3 and 6?

10. What is the greatest common factor of 21 and 35?

11. What is the greatest common factor of 7 and 14?

12. What is the greatest common factor of 24 and 40?

13. What is the greatest common factor of 3 and 5?

14. What is the greatest common factor of 60 and 100?

15. What is the greatest common factor of 63 and 84?

16. What is the greatest common factor of 54 and 72?

17. What is the greatest common factor of 54 and 90?

18. What is the greatest common factor of 20 and 30?

19. What is the greatest common factor of 2 and 4?

20. What is the greatest common factor of 27 and 36?

21. What is the greatest common factor of 72 and 96?

22. What is the greatest common factor of 6 and 10?

23. What is the greatest common factor of 10 and 20?

24. What is the greatest common factor of 81 and 108?

25. What is the greatest common factor of 36 and 48?

26. What is the greatest common factor of 27 and 45?

27. What is the greatest common factor of 18 and 30?

28. What is the greatest common factor of 90 and 120?

29. What is the greatest common factor of 12 and 18?

30. What is the greatest common factor of 45 and 60?

31. What is the greatest common factor of 6 and 12?

32. What is the greatest common factor of 4 and 6?

33. What is the greatest common factor of 12 and 20?

34. What is the greatest common factor of 14 and 21?

35. What is the greatest common factor of 9 and 18?

36. What is the greatest common factor of 16 and 24?

37. What is the greatest common factor of 8 and 12?

38. What is the greatest common factor of 10 and 15?

39. What is the greatest common factor of 24 and 40?

40. What is the greatest common factor of 18 and 30?

3. LEAST COMMON MULTIPLE

1. What is the least common multiple of 21 and 63?

2. What is the least common multiple of 5 and 25?

3. What is the least common multiple of 1 and 2?

4. What is the least common multiple of 27 and 81?

5. What is the least common multiple of 8 and 16?

6. What is the least common multiple of 24 and 72?

7. What is the least common multiple of 6 and 12?

8. What is the least common multiple of 7 and 35?

9. What is the least common multiple of 14 and 28?

10. What is the least common multiple of 2 and 6?

11. What is the least common multiple of 5 and 10?

12. What is the least common multiple of 7 and 14?

13. What is the least common multiple of 15 and 45?

14. What is the least common multiple of 18 and 54?

15. What is the least common multiple of 2 and 4?

16. What is the least common multiple of 10 and 20?

17. What is the least common multiple of 1 and 3?

18. What is the least common multiple of 9 and 45?

19. What is the least common multiple of 20 and 40?

20. What is the least common multiple of 18 and 36?

21. What is the least common multiple of 3 and 6?

22. What is the least common multiple of 9 and 27?

23. What is the least common multiple of 4 and 20?

24. What is the least common multiple of 10 and 30?

25. What is the least common multiple of 8 and 16?

26. What is the least common multiple of 3 and 9?

27. What is the least common multiple of 10 and 50?

28. What is the least common multiple of 8 and 24?

29. What is the least common multiple of 9 and 18?

30. What is the least common multiple of 4 and 8?

31. What is the least common multiple of 10 and 20?

32. What is the least common multiple of 4 and 12?

33. What is the least common multiple of 6 and 18?

34. What is the least common multiple of 6 and 12?

35. What is the least common multiple of 3 and 15?

36. What is the least common multiple of 7 and 21?

37. What is the least common multiple of 30 and 90?

38. What is the least common multiple of 8 and 40?

39. What is the least common multiple of 12 and 36?

40. What is the least common multiple of 16 and 32?

4. PRIME OR COMPOSITE NUMBERS

1. Is 82 a prime or a composite number?
   a) Composite
   b) Prime

2. Is 44 a prime or a composite number?
   a) Composite
   b) Prime

3. Is 66 a prime or a composite number?
   a) Composite
   b) Prime

4. Is 17 a prime or a composite number?
   a) Prime
   b) Composite

5. Is 21 a prime or a composite number?
   a) Composite
   b) Prime

6. Is 79 a prime or a composite number?
   a) Prime
   b) Composite

7. Is 60 a prime or a composite number?
   a) Composite
   b) Prime

8. Is 36 a prime or a composite number?
   a) Composite
   b) Prime

9. Is 43 a prime or a composite number?
   a) Prime
   b) Composite

10. Is 13 a prime or a composite number?
    a) Prime
    b) Composite

11. Match the prime and composite numbers
    72   Prime number
    71   Composite number

12. Is 71 a prime or a composite number?
    a) Prime
    b) Composite

13. Is 83 a prime or a composite number?
    a) Prime
    b) Composite

14. Is 31 a prime or a composite number?
    a) Prime
    b) Composite

15. Is 59 a prime or a composite number?
   a) Prime
   b) Composite

16. Match the prime and composite numbers
   27   Prime number
   97   Composite number

17. Is 3 a prime or a composite number?
   a) Prime
   b) Composite

18. Is 45 a prime or a composite number?
   a) Composite
   b) Prime

19. Is 75 a prime or a composite number?
   a) Composite
   b) Prime

20. Is 27 a prime or a composite number?
   a) Composite
   b) Prime

22. Is 62 a prime or a composite number?
   a) Composite
   b) Prime

21. Is 51 a prime or a composite number?
   a) Composite
   b) Prime

23. Is 68 a prime or a composite number?
   a) Composite
   b) Prime

24. Is 81 a prime or a composite number?
   a) Composite
   b) Prime

25. Is 29 a prime or a composite number?
   a) Prime
   b) Composite

26. Match the prime and composite numbers
   84   Prime number
   83   Composite number

27. Is 7 a prime or a composite number?
   a) Prime
   b) Composite

28. Is 8 a prime or a composite number?
   a) Composite
   b) Prime

29. Is 77 a prime or a composite number?
   a) Composite
   b) Prime

30. Is 87 a prime or a composite number?
   a) Composite
   b) Prime

31. Is 2 a prime or a composite number?
   a) Prime
   b) Composite

32. Is 20 a prime or a composite number?
   a) Composite
   b) Prime

33. Is 78 a prime or a composite number?
   a) Composite
   b) Prime

34. Is 10 a prime or a composite number?
   a) Composite
   b) Prime

35. Is 53 a prime or a composite number?
   a) Prime
   b) Composite

36. Match the prime and composite numbers
   42   Prime number
   41   Composite number

37. Is 16 a prime or a composite number?
   a) Composite
   b) Prime

38. Match the prime and composite numbers
   51   Prime number
   59   Composite number

39. Is 4 a prime or a composite number?
   a) Composite
   b) Prime

40. Match the prime and composite numbers
   22   Prime number
   11   Composite number

5. SQUARE OF A NUMBER

1. What is the square of 6?

2. What is the square of 37?

3. What is the square of 29?

4. What is the square of 39?

5. What is the square of 19?

6. What is the square of 32?

7. What is the square of 27?

8. What is the square of 42?

9. What is the square of 3?

10. What is the square of 15?

11. What is the square of 11?

12. What is the square of 38?

13. What is the square of 45?

14. What is the square of 41?

15. What is the square of 5?

16. What is the square of 10?

17. What is the square of 48?

18. What is the square of 34?

19. What is the square of 26?

20. What is the square of 21?

21. What is the square of 14?

22. What is the square of 30?

23. What is the square of 43?

24. What is the square of 18?

25. What is the square of 31?

26. What is the square of 20?

27. What is the square of 23?

28. What is the square of 40?

29. What is the square of 24?

30. What is the square of 44?

31. What is the square of 35?

32. What is the square of 12?

33. What is the square of 13?

34. What is the square of 47?

35. What is the square of 25?

36. What is the square of 7?

37. What is the square of 50?

38. What is the square of 28?

39. What is the square of 49?

40. What is the square of 17?

6. SQUARE ROOT OF A NUMBER

1. What is the square root of 25?

2. What is the square root of 1681?

3. What is the square root of 196?

4. What is the square root of 1024?

5. What is the square root of 1849?

6. What is the square root of 1936?

7. What is the square root of 81?

8. What is the square root of 9?

9. What is the square root of 625?

10. What is the square root of 289?

11. What is the square root of 900?

12. What is the square root of 529?

13. What is the square root of 1296?

14. What is the square root of 225?

15. What is the square root of 36?

16. What is the square root of 1600?

17. What is the square root of 1444?

18. What is the square root of 961?

19. What is the square root of 49?

20. What is the square root of 1089?

21. What is the square root of 400?

22. What is the square root of 729?

23. What is the square root of 169?

24. What is the square root of 121?

25. What is the square root of 324?

26. What is the square root of 100?

27. What is the square root of 441?

28. What is the square root of 484?

29. What is the square root of 784?

30. What is the square root of 16?

31. What is the square root of 4?

32. What is the square root of 256?

33. What is the square root of 1764?

34. What is the square root of 1521?

35. What is the square root of 576?

36. What is the square root of 64?

37. What is the square root of 144?

38. What is the square root of 361?

39. What is the square root of 1156?

40. What is the square root of 1225?

7. NUMBER THEORY (TRUE OR FALSE)

Verify whether each of the following statement is correct (true) or not (false)?

1. The square of 8 is 64
   a) True
   b) False

2. The square root of 25 is 5
   a) True
   b) False

3. The square of 4 is 16
   a) True
   b) False

4. The square root of 16 is 4
   a) True
   b) False

5. The square root of 100 is 10
   a) True
   b) False

6. The greatest common factor of 15 and 25 is 5
   a) True
   b) False

7. The square root of 36 is 6
   a) True
   b) False

8. The greatest common factor of 27 and 45 is 9
   a) True
   b) False

9. The square of 9 is 3
   a) False
   b) True

10. The square root of 4 is 2
    a) True
    b) False

11. The least common multiple of 12 and 20 is 60
    a) True
    b) False

12. The square of 64 is 8
    False
    True

13. The greatest common factor of 24 and 40 is 120
    a) False
    b) True

14. The square of 36 is 6
    a) False
    b) True

15. The greatest common factor of 21 and 35 is 7
    a) True
    b) False

16. The square root of 6 is 36
    a) False
    b) True

17. The square of 25 is 5
    a) False
    b) True

18. The least common multiple of 18 and 30 is 90
    a) True
    b) False

19. The least common multiple of 9 and 15 is 45
    a) True
    b) False

20. The square root of 3 is 9
    a) False
    b) True

21. The least common multiple of 27 and 45 is 135
    a) True
    b) False

22. The greatest common factor of 24 and 40 is 8
    a) True
    b) False

23. The greatest common factor of 3 and 5 is 1
    a) True
    b) False

24. The square root of 2 is 4
    a) True
    b) False

25. The square root of 49 is 7
    True
    False

26. The least common multiple of 24 and 40 is 8
    a) False
    b) True

27. The square of 16 is 4
    a) False
    b) True

28. The square root of 4 is 2
    a) True
    b) False

29. The square root of 7 is 49
   a) False
   b) True

30. The square of 5 is 25
   a) True
   b) False

31. The greatest common factor of 27 and 45 is 135
   a) False
   b) True

32. The square root of 9 is 3
   a) True
   b) False

33. The square root of 1 is 2
   a) True
   b) False

34. The least common multiple of 27 and 45 is 9
   a) False
   b) True

35. The greatest common factor of 3 and 5 is 1
   a) True
   b) False

36. The greatest common factor of 15 and 25 is 5
   a) True
   b) False

37. The greatest common factor of 18 and 30 is 6
   a) True
   b) False

38. The greatest common factor of 21 and 35 is 105
   a) False
   b) True

39. The least common multiple of 6 and 10 is 30
   a) True
   b) False

40. The square root of 9 is 81
   a) False
   b) True

8. DETERMINE RATIO

1. There are 17 roses and 10 sunflowers in the garden. Ratio of sunflowers to total flowers is
   a) 10:17
   b) 17:10
   c) 10:27

2. There are 20 girls and 5 boys in a chorus. What is the ratio of girls to boys?
   a) 4:1
   b) 20:25
   c) 5:20

3. 25:100 can also be represented as
   a) 1:4
   b) 2:04
   c) 3:04

4. There are 12 roses and 16 sunflowers in the garden. Ratio of roses to sunflowers is
   a) 12:11
   b) 3:4
   c) 3:7

5. 200:100 can also be represented as
   a) 2:1
   b) 1:02
   c) 4:02

6. 5:100 can also be represented as
   a) 20:1
   b) 1:20
   c) 2:10

7. There are 16 girls and 32 boys in a class. What is the ratio of boys to girls?
   a) 1:2
   b) 2:1
   c) 1:4

8. There are 20 men and 25 women in a party. What is the ratio of women to total people in the party?
   a) 20:25
   b) 4:5
   c) 5:9

9. There are 12 girls and 5 boys in a class. What is the ratio of girls to total kids?
   a) 12:05
   b) 5:12
   c) 12:17

10. 250:100 can also be represented as
    a) 5:2
    b) 4:03
    c) 5:03

11. 250:150 can also be represented as
   a) 2:1
   b) 5:3
   c) 3:5

12. 44:99 can also be represented as
   a) 1:9
   b) 4:9
   c) 4:1

13. There are 8 red roses and 20 white roses in the garden. What is the ratio of white roses to red roses?
   a) 2:4
   b) 2:5
   c) 2:10

14. 3:5 can also be represented as
   a) 2:05
   b) 1:02
   c) 15:25

15. There are 12 girls and 5 boys in a class. What is the ratio of girls to boys?
   a) 12:5
   b) 5:12
   c) 12:17

16. There are 20 dark chocolates and 5 white chocolates in a box. What is the ratio of white chocolates to total number of chocolates in the box?
   a) 1:5
   b) 2:5
   c) 5:20

17. There are 27 cards and 27 envelopes in a box of greeting cards. Ratio of cards to envelopes is
   a) 1:1
   b) 7:1
   c) 1:7

18. There are 12 oranges and 5 apples in a basket. What is the ratio of apples to oranges?
   a) 12:5
   b) 5:12
   c) 12:17

19. If Rick drives 14 miles and Tom drives 21 miles every day. Find the ratio of miles driven by Rick and Tom every day.
   a) 4:3
   b) 2:3
   c) 1:3

20. A group of workers made 27 miles of the road on Monday and 36 miles of the road on Tuesday. Find the ratio of the road made by the group of workers on Monday and Tuesday.
   a) 3:4
   b) 7:3
   c) 7:4

21. 7:10 can also be represented as
   a) 14:20
   b) 5:10
   c) 10:20

22. 50:75 can also be represented as
   a) 2:3
   b) 10:5
   c) 5:10

23. 5/7 can be represented in ratio as
   a) 5:2
   b) 5:7
   c) 7:5

24. Richard's grandma made 20 cookie and 35 apple pies on Christmas. Find the ratio of apple pies to the total number of items made by grandma.
   a) 4:7
   b) 7:11
   c) 7:4

25. Mike's dad goes to his office by car and then take bus. If he travels 6 miles by car and 36 miles by bus. What ratio of the total distance, he covers by car ?
   a) 1:7
   b) 1:6
   c) 6:7

26. There are 24 roses and 18 sunflowers in a bouquet. What is the ratio of sunflowers to roses?
   a) 3:4
   b) 6:4
   c) 2:3

27. There are 48 paintings and 36 sculptures in a museum. Find the ratio of paintings to sculptures.
   a) 8:4
   b) 12:3
   c) 4:3

28. 16:40 can also be represented as
   a) 2:5
   b) 1:3
   c) 1:4

29. There are 12 pineapples and 5 apples in a fruit basket. What is the ratio of apples to pineapples?
   a) 12:5
   b) 5:12
   c) 12:17

30. There are 35 black marbles and 25 red marbles in a jar. What is the ratio of black marbles to the total number of marbles in the jar?
   a) 7:12
   b) 17:10
   c) 7:5

9. UNDERSTAND PERCENTAGE CONCEPT

Write the right percentage value for a given number.

1. 100 % of 100 = _____

2. 90 % of 340 = _____

3. 90 % of 5140 = _____

4. 70 % of 820 = _____

5. 80 % of 3220 = _____

6. 20 % of 4660 = _____

7. 50 % of 3940 = _____

8. 10 % of 2500 = _____

9. 60 % of 1060 = _____

10. 80 % of 5380 = _____

11. 50 % of 1300 = _____

12. 50 % of 100 = _____

13. 60 % of 3700 = _____

14. 90 % of 2980 = _____

15. 40 % of 4180 = _____

16. 70 % of 5620 = _____

17. 30 % of 4420 = _____

18. 60 % of 5860 = _____

19. 50 % of 6100 = _____

20. 30 % of 1780 = _____

21. 10 % of 4900 = _____

22. 80 % of 580 = _____

23. 100 % of 2740 = _____

24. 10 % of 2260 = _____

25. 70 % of 3460 = _____

26. 40 % of 1540 = _____

27. 40 % of 6340 = _____

28. 20 % of 2020 = _____

10. COMPARE AND BALANCE PERCENTAGE VALUES

Compare the following percentage value by placing the right comparison sign > or = <:

1. 10% of 100 _____ 2% of 200

2. 20% of 200 _____ 40% of 100

3. 100 % of 200 _____1% of 1000000

4. 10% of 100 _____ 40% of 20

5. 20% of 1000 _____ 50% of 200

6. 20% of 100 _____ 40% of 100

7. 200% of 100 _____ 300% of 100

8. 10% of 100 _____ 20% of 40

9. 25% of 1000 _____ 25% of 100

10. 150% of 100 _____ 100% of 100

11. 25% of 100 _____ 10% of 100

12. 10% of 100 _____ 5% of 200

13. 10% of 100 _____ 2% of 200

14. 1% of 300 _____ 2 % 400

15. 25% of 100 _____ 10% of 100

16. 20% of 1000 _____ 50% of 200

17. 10% of 100 _____ 50% of 20

18. 20% of 100 _____ 50% of 20

19. 100 % of 200 _____1% of 2000000

20. 1 % of 200 _____1% of 100

21. 10% of 100 ____ 40% of 20

22. 10% of 100 ____ 25% of 40

23. 150% of 100 ____ 100% of 100

24. 10% of 100 ____ 25% of 40

25. 20% of 100 ____ 40% of 100

26. 200% of 100 ____ 300% of 100

27. 200% of 100 ____ 100% of 100

28. 25% of 1000 ____ 25% of 100

29. 1 % of 200 ____ 1% of 100

30. 1% of 300 ____ 2 % 200

31. 25% of 100 ____ 10% of 100

32. 1% of 300 ____ 2 % 200

33. 1% of 300 ____ 2 % 400

34. 10% of 100 ____ 5% of 200

35. 20% of 100 ____ 50% of 20

36. 25% of 100 ____ 10% of 100

37. 10% of 100 ____ 20% of 40

38. 20% of 200 ____ 40% of 100

39. 10% of 100 ____ 50% of 20

40. 200% of 100 ____ 100% of 100

11.   FRACTION, RATIO AND PERCENTAGE (TRUE OR FALSE)

Verify whether each of the following statement is correct (true) or not (false)?

1. 21:30 is equivalent to 41:60
    a) False
    b) True

2. 3/9 < 1/9
    a) False
    b) True

3. 12:13 is equivalent to 14:15
    a) False
    b) True

4. 5:3 is equivalent to 10:6
    a) False
    b) True

5. 1/100 > 1/10
    a) False
    b) True

6. 2/ 10 < 1/5
    a) False
    b) True

7. 5 % 0f 500 is 25
    a) False
    b) True

8. 1/5 > -1/5
    a) False
    b) True

9. 3/3 < 2000/3000
    a) False
    b) True

10. 2/ 10 < 1/5
    a) False
    b) True

11. 1/13 > 1/26
    a) False
    b) True

12. 0 > 1/5
    a) False
    b) True

13. 2:3 is equivalent to 10:15
    a) False
    b) True

14. 2:30 is equivalent to 4:80
    a) False
    b) True

15. 4/5 > 2/5
   a) False
   b) True

16. 5/1 > 1/5
   a) False
   b) True

17. 20 % of 5 is 1
   a) False
   b) True

18. 25 % 0f 500 is 125
   a) False
   b) True

19. 100/200 > 1/5
   a) False
   b) True

20. 51 % 0f 500 is 255
   a) False
   b) True

21. 1/13 > 1/26
   a) False
   b) True

22. 0 > -1/5
   a) False
   b) True

23. 51 % 0f 100 is 51
   a) False
   b) True

24. 25 % 0f 100 is 25
   a) False
   b) True

25. 2:13 is equivalent to 4:26
   a) False
   b) True

26. 100 % 0f 500 is 100
   a) False
   b) True

27. 50% of 400 is 200
   a) False
   b) True

28. 21 % 0f 200 is 42
   a) False
   b) True

29. 3/5 > -3/5
   a) False
   b) True

30. 1/10 < 1/100
   a) False
   b) True

31. 1/2 > 0
  a) False
  b) True

36. 0 > 1/5
  a) False
  b) True

32. 5 % 0f 500 is 5
  a) False
  b) True

37. 20% of 100 is 20
  a) False
  b) True

33. 2:3 is equivalent to 10:15
  a) False
  b) True

38. 1/2 > 0
  a) False
  b) True

34. 40/90 < 90/40
  a) False
  b) True

39. 1/100 > 1/10
  a) False
  b) True

35. 1/5 > -1/5
  a) False
  b) True

40. 0 > 1/5
  a) False
  b) True

12.   FRACTION, RATIO AND PERCENTAGE (WORD PROBLEMS)

1.   There are 17 rose plants and 8 sunflower plants in a garden. What is the ratio of rose plants to total number of plants in the garden?
   a) 8:17
   b) 17:08
   c) 8:25

2.   1:100 can also be represented as
   a) 1 %
   b) 0.1 %
   c) 10%

3.   Sam's age is 1/4 of his dad's age. If his dad is 40 years, how many years is Sam's dad older than Sam?
   a) 30 years
   b) 10 years

4.   There are 20 girls and 5 boys in a chorus. What is the ratio of boys to girls?
   a) 20:05
   b) 20:25
   c) 1:4

5.   What is 10% of 200?
   a) 1
   b) 10
   c) 20

6.   Mary made 2 types of cookies. She used 2/3 pound of sugar to chocolate chip cookie and 1/3 pound in another one. How much sugar did she use in total?
   a) 1 pound
   b) 2/3 pound

7. Rick got a box of 100 candies. 1/5 of candies were blue and rest of them were red. How many were red candies in the box?
    a) 20
    b) 80

8. 3:5 can also be represented as
    a) 2:05
    b) 1:02
    c) 15:25

9. If Lisa's age is 1/3rd of her mom. What is the age of Lisa's mom if Lisa is 20 years old?
    a) 40 years
    b) 60 years

10. What is 1% of 400?
    a) 4
    b) 40
    c) 20

11. 1/3 of the mangoes were sour. If the box had 30 mangoes, how many were not sour?
    a) 10
    b) 20

12. Lucas collected around 600 candies on Halloween. If he ate 2/3 of the candies and donated the remaining. How many candies did he donate?
    a) 200
    b) 400

13. Johnathan walked 1/4 mile to school. He walked another 1/4 mile from school to the playground. He walked another 1/2 mile back to his home. How many miles did he walk in total?

14. What is 10% of 400?
   a) 1
   b) 40
   c) 20

15. There are 20 girls and 5 boys in a chorus. What is the ratio of girls to boys?
   a) 4:1
   b) 20:25
   c) 5:20

16. There are 12 boys and 5 girls in a birthday party. What is the ratio of girls to total kids in the party?
   a) 12:5
   b) 5:12
   c) 5:17

17. What is 1% of 200?
   a) 2
   b) 10
   c) 20

18. There are 27 blue marbles and 36 red marbles in a box. What is the ratio of blue marbles to total number of marbles?
   a) 3:7
   b) 3:1
   c) 3:4

19. If Monica's age is 1/3rd the age of her mom's age. What is the age of Monica if her mom is 60 years old?
   a) 20 years
   b) 40 years

20. Richa made 2 types of pizza for dinner. She used 1/3 pounds of flour in one and 5/6 pounds in another one. How much flour did she use in total?

21. 200:100 can also be represented as
   a) 2:1
   b) 1:02
   c) 4:02

22. Greg's dad is 1/2 of his grandpa. Greg's age is 1/4 of his dad. If Greg's age is 10 years. What is his grandpa's age?
   a) 40
   b) 80

23. Esha received a gift of chocolate box on her birthday. There are 100 chocolate candies in the box. 1/5 of candies are dark cholates and rest are white milk cholates candies. How many candies are white milk candies?
   a) 20
   b) 80

24. Elton received $100 in prize in spelling bee contest in his school. He bought a toy for his sister and he paid 1/4th the award money to buy the toy. How much money did he have left with?
   a) 75
   b) 25

25. There are 8 bananas and 17 apples in a fruit basket. What it the ratio of apples to bananas?
   a) 8:17
   b) 17:8
   c) 8:25

26. Sam's age is 1/4 of his dad's age. If his dad is 40 years old. what is Sam's age?

27. 350:25 can also be represented as
   a) 70:25
   b) 7:1
   c) 7:25

28. There are 100 pebbles in a box. 1/4 of the pebbles are blue, 1/4 of the pebbles are yellow and remaining are Red. How many are red?
   a) 50
   b) 25

29. If a boy ate 1/3 of a cookie. How much cookie is still remaining to be finished?
   a) 2/3
   b) 1/3

30. What is 1% of 300?
   a) 3
   b) 60
   c) 30

31. If a boy finished 2/3 of a pizza. How much pizza is still remaining?
   a) 1/3
   b) 1/2
   c) 2/3

32. You have been saving for a Spiderman game on Game Box which costs $100. If You have already collected 3/4 of the cost. How much money do you need more to buy the game?

33. In a national swim team, there are 12 girls from California, 10 girls from Ohio, 5 boys from California and 6 boys from Ohio. What is the ratio of boys to girls in the team?
    a) 2:1
    b) 5:12
    c) 1:2

34. What is 20% of 200?
    a) 40
    b) 10
    c) 20

35. If 4/5 of glass is full of water. How much glass is empty?
    a) 1/4
    b) 1/5
    c) 4/5

36. Tom walked 1/3 mile to his school. After school, he went another 1/3 mile to the playground. His home is approx. 2/3 mile from the playground. How many miles did he travel all day?

37. What is 4% of 400?

38. Arun went on trekking for around 2 miles and then took another route to reach home which was around 1/2 of the distance which he travelled earlier. How many miles did he walk in total?

13. RELATIONSHIP BETWEEN RATIO, PERCENTAGE AND FRACTION

1. Ratio 8:25 can also be represented as
   a) 8/17
   b) 17/8
   c) 8/25

2. Fraction 20/5 can also be represented as
   a) 4:1
   b) 20:25
   c) 5:20

3. Ratio 4:16 can also be represented as
   a) 6/10
   b) 3/4
   c) 1/4

4. Ratio 5:20 can also be represented as
   a) 5 %
   b) 20 %
   c) 25 %

5. Fraction 20/25 can also be represented as
   a) 20:05
   b) 4:5
   c) 5:20

6. Ratio 8:40 can also be represented as
   a) 20 %
   b) 8 %
   c) 40 %

7. Ratio 10:27 can also be represented as
   a) 10/17
   b) 17/10
   c) 10/27

8. Ratio 1:4 can also be represented as
   a) 6/10
   b) 3/4
   c) 1/4

9. Fraction 12/36 can also be represented as
   a) 12:05
   b) 5:12
   c) 1:3

10. Ratio 8:16 can also be represented as
    a) 50 %
    b) 8 %
    c) 16 %

11. Ratio 20:5 can also be represented as
    a) 400 %
    b) 20 %
    c) 5 %

12. Ratio 14:20 can also be represented as
    a) 70 %
    b) 50 %
    c) 40 %

13. Fraction 17/8 can also be represented as
 a) 8:17
 b) 17:8
 c) 8:25

14. Ratio 200:100 can also be represented as
 a) 2/1
 b) 1/2
 c) 4/2

15. Ratio 5:7 can also be represented as
 a) 5/2
 b) 5/7
 c) 7/5

16. Ratio 8:25 can also be represented as
 a) 8/17
 b) 17/8
 c) 8/25

17. Ratio 20:5 can also be represented as
 a) 4/1
 b) 20/25
 c) 5/20

18. Ratio 25:100 can also be represented as
 a) 1/4
 b) 2/4
 c) 3/4

19. Ratio 250:100 can also be represented as
 5/2
 4/3
 5/3

20. Ratio 5:25 can also be represented as
 a) 20 %
 b) 5 %
 c) 30 %

21. Ratio 17:10 can also be represented as
 a) 10/17
 b) 17/10
 c) 10/27

22. Ratio 17:34 can also be represented as
 a) 17 %
 b) 50 %
 c) 34 %

23. Ratio 17:10 can also be represented as
 a) 10/17
 b) 17/10
 c) 10/27

24. Fraction 20/25 can also be represented as
 a) 20:05
 b) 4:5
 c) 5:20

25. Ratio 10:100 can also be represented as
    a) 10 %
    b) 100 %
    c) 110 %

26. Ratio 1:100 can also be represented as
    a) 1 %
    b) 10 %
    c) 110 %

27. Ratio 8:32 can also be represented as
    a) 20 %
    b) 8 %
    c) 25 %

28. Fraction 7:14 can also be represented as
    a) 50%
    b) 5:7
    c) 7:05

29. Fraction 5/12 can also be represented as
    a) 12:05
    b) 5:12
    c) 12:17

30. Ratio 5:20 can also be represented as
    a) 1/4
    b) 4/1
    c) 20/5

37. Fraction 20/5 can also be represented as
   a) 20:5
   b) 20:25
   c) 5:20

38. Ratio 5:20 can also be represented as
   a) 20/5
   b) 20/25
   c) 5/20

39. Fraction 12/17 can also be represented as
   a) 12:05
   b) 5:12
   c) 12:17

40. Ratio 17:8 can also be represented as
   a) 8/17
   b) 17/8
   c) 8/25

14. WRITE MATHEMATICAL EXPRESSIONS AND EQUATIONS

Write or choose mathematical expressions or equations for the following problems:

1. a is divided by 8
   a) a/8
   b) 8a

2. Number n is divided by 20 and add 12 to the result
   a) n/20+12
   b) (n/20) +12

3. Twice of x is equal to 2
   a) 2 x =2
   b) x =2

4. a is increased by 9
   a) a+9
   b) 9-a

5. A times A
   a) A + A
   b) A x A

6. Andy has 10 cards more than Nick. If Nick has x number of cards. What is the correct expression to show how many cards Andy has?
   a) x +10
   b) 10- x

7. Product of n, 10 and 27/2
   a) 270/3/ x
   b) n x 10 x 27/2

8. The quotient of 18 and n
   a) 8/n
   b) n/18

9. Product of 97, m, and w
   a) 97 x m x w
   b) mw/97

10. Cube of t
    a) t x t x t
    b) 3 x t

11. 5 times of a number n
    a) 5n
    b) n/5

12. Product of A, 10 and 27
    a) A x 10 x 27
    b) 270/ x

13. The sum of q and 8
    a) q+8
    b) 8-q

14. The sum of 7, n, and 10
   a) 7+n+10
   b) n+10

15. 2 is added to a number n
   a) n2
   b) n+2

16. Twice of x plus 5 equal to 5
   a) 2 x + 5 = 2
   b) x + 5 = 2

17. The quotient of 14 and 7
   a) 14/7
   b) 7/14

18. The product of 8 and 10
   a) 8 x 10
   b) 10/8

19. A number n is divided by 2 is equal to 10
   a) n/2 = 10
   b) 2n = 10

20. b times 3
   a) b x b x b
   b) b x 3

21. Divide a number n by 20 and add 10 to the result
   a) n/20 + 10
   b) (20/n) +10

22. The difference between 10 and 5
   a) 10 - 5
   b) 10+5

23. The difference of 5 and s
   a) 5-s
   b) s+5

24. Multiply a number n by 20 and add 100
   a) n/20+100
   b) 20n +100

25. 2 is added to a number a and the result is divided by 3
   a) 2/3+n
   b) (2+n)/3

15.   VALUE OF UNKNOWN EXPRESSION IN MATHEMATICAL EQUATIONS

Find the value of unknown variable in the following equations:

1. $x + 23 = 2 + 2x$

2. $5 + X = 81$

3. $2y + 20 = 40 + 4y$

4. $20 / K = 40$

5. $10 / Y = 5$

6. $u + 20 = 5u - 2$

7. $10 \times Y = 5$

8. $u + 20 = 2u - 2$

9. $20 - X = 20$

10. $x + 23 = 2 + 4x$

11. $x + 23 = 2 + 3x$

12. $20 - 3X = 19$

13. $5 + X = 8 - 12X$

14. $20 / Y - 20 = 40$

15. $X + 123 = 125 - 2X$

16. $10 / Y = 50$

17. $5 + X = 8$

18. $3x = 45 - 12x$

19. $28 - Y = 20$

20. $2Y + 123 = 125$

21. 20 / K = 4

22. u + 20 = 2u - 21

23. 20 - X = 19

24. 2y = 50 - 3y

25. X + 127 = 129

16.   SOLVE MATHEMATICAL EQUATIONS USING MULTIPLE OPERATIONS

Solve the following mathematical expressions:

1. 5 x 5 (25/ 6) x 36 (1/6) + 23 = _____

11. 2 x 4 (3/4) + 2 (30/2) = _____

2. 10 x 2(3-4) = _____

12. 2 x 3 (2 /3) - 14 = _____

3. 5 x 5 (25/ 6) x 36 (1/6) = _____

13. 3 (10 + 2) - 12 = _____

4. 3 x 5(17/5) - 51 = _____

14. 2 x (5-6) + 230 = _____

5. 3 (10 + 2) + 22 = _____

15. 2 x (5-6) + 23 (1+2) = _____

6. 3 x 5(17/5) + 51 = _____

16. 2 x (5+6) - 13 = _____

7. 2 x 4 (3/4) + 2 (3/2) = _____

17. 10/ (8 + 2) + 22 = _____

8. 2 x 4 (3/4) - 2 (3/2) = _____

18. 3 (10 + 2) + 220 = _____

9. 2 x (5-6) + 23 = _____

19. 2 x 5 - 6 + 23 = _____

10. 3 x 5(17/5) - 51 (10 + 3) = _____

20. 10 x 2(3+4) = _____

21. 5 x 6 (25/ 6) x 6 (1/6) = _____

22. 3 x 5(17/5) - 5 (2 + 3) = _____

23. 3 x 5(17/5) - 51 (21 - 3) = _____

24. 2 x 3 (2 /3) +14 = _____

25. 3 x 8 (25/ 5) x 36 (1/36) = _____

17.   SOLVE MATHEMATICAL EQUATIONS (TRUE OR FALSE)

Verify whether each of the following expressions is correct (true) or not (false)?

1. 2 x (5-6) + 230 = 444
    a) False
    b) True

2. 2 x (5-6) + 23 (1+2) = 33
    a) False
    b) True

3. 3 (10 + 2) + 22 = 43
    a) False
    b) True

4. 3 (10 + 2) + 220 = 222
    a) False
    b) True

5. 2 x 3 (2 /3) +14 = 18
    a) True
    b) False

6. 10 x 2(3+4) = 140
    a) True
    b) False

7. 3 (10 + 2) + 22 = 58
    a) True
    b) False

8. 3 x 5(17/5) - 5 (2 + 3) = 32
    a) False
    b) True

9. 10 x 2(3-4) = -20
    a) True
    b) False

10. 2 x (5-6) + 23 = 21
    a) True
    b) False

11. 2 x (5-6) + 23 = 22
    a) False
    b) True

12. 2 x (5+6) - 13 = 9
    a) True
    b) False

13. 2 x 4 (3/4) + 2 (30/2) = 32
    a) False
    b) True

14. 2 x 4 (3/4) + 2 (3/2) = 9
    a) True
    b) False

15.   3 (10 + 2) - 12 = 24
   a) True
   b) False

16.   3 x 5(17/5) - 51 (21 - 3) = 43
   a) False
   b) True

17.   5 x 5 (25/ 6) x 36 (1/6) =625
   a) True
   b) False

18.   5 x 5 (25/ 6) x 36 (1/6) + 23 = 625
   a) False
   b) True

19.   3 x 5(17/5) - 51 = 0
   a) True
   b) False

20.   2 x 4 (3/4) - 2 (3/2) = 4
   a) True
   b) False

21.   5 x 5 (25/ 6) x 36 (1/36) = 5555
   a) False
   b) True

22.   3 x 5(17/5) - 51 (10 + 3) = 33
   a) False
   b) True

23.   3 x 5(17/5) + 51 = 102
   a) True
   b) False

24.   5 x 5 (25/ 6) x 36 (1/6) = 800
   a) False
   b) True

25.   2 x 3 (2 /3) - 14 = -10
   a) True
   b) False

18.   DETERMINE UNIT PRICE OF AN OBJECT

1.   100-gallons milk cost $400. What is the price of milk per gallon?

2.   There are 100 hats in a bundle for $120. Find out the price of 1 hat?

3.   If 10 notebooks cost $13 in wholesale. What would be the average price of 1 notebook?

4.   If 50 box units cost $25. What is the price per box?

5.   Rick bought 30 gallons of paint for $60. Calculate the price of 1 gallon.

6.   If the price of 30 basketballs is $120. What is the price of 1 basketball?

7.   If the price of 2 kilograms of popcorn is $8 in a grocery store. What would be price of 1/2 kilogram of popcorn?

8.   In a retail outlet, 25 pots cost $500. What is the cost of a single pot?

9.   If 40 candies are sold for $20. What is the unit price of a candy?

10.   In a wholesale market, price of 100 T-Shirts is $2000. What is the unit price of each T-Shirt?

11. Mike bought 8 work books for $24 at a bookstore. Find out the price of each work book.

12. Lisa has 3 sons. She bought 3 ice-creams for $4.50 for her sons. What is price of each ice-cream?

13. What is the price of 1 drumstick if 20 drumsticks cost $22?

14. Raman's dad bought 12 goody bags on his birthday to give his friends. If he spent $30. What is the price of each goody bag?

15. A cartoon of 100 water bottles of 1 gallon each is priced for $23. What is unit price of water bottle?

16. If the cost of 100 yards' cloth is $45. What is the price for 10 yards?

17. Amit bought 5 apples and 6 oranges for $33. Find the average price of one fruit?

18. Jonathan bought 3 pairs of pants and 3 shirts for $25? What is the price of each unit?

19. Tom bought 20 donuts and a dozen bagels for a seminar and paid $44 to the shopkeeper. What is the average price of one item?

20. Justin paid $86 for a pair of shoes and 2 pairs of slippers? What is the average of each item?

21. In Chicago, price of 2 soft toys is $60. In Naperville, same toy is priced at $40 for each toy. Where will you get a better deal?
  a) Chicago
  b) Naperville

22. At a paint store, 30 gallons of paint cost $60, and 60 gallons of paint cost $100. Which price is better?
  a) 60 gallons
  b) 30 gallons

23. A pack of 100 hats at a wholesale store is priced for $120, and a pack of $50 hats is priced for $80. Which is a better price?
  a) 100 hats pack
  b) 50 hats pack

24. In a mall, price of 100 yards of cloth is $45, same cloth is also available in small cut pieces. If 10 yards' piece is priced at $4. Which is a better deal?
  a) 100 yards
  b) 10 yards

25. At a chocolate parlor, 20 candies pack is for $10 and 30 candies pack is available for $12. Which is a better deal?
  a) 20 Candies for $10
  b) 30 candies for $12

26. At a garden palace, price of 10 pots is listed as $45. If you buy 5, you have to pay $25. Which is a better deal?
  a) 10 for $45
  b) 5 for $25

19.   DETERMINE COST MULTIPLE OBJECTS

1.   If a pack of 100 hats cost $100. What is the cost of a pair of hats?

2.   At a grocery store, a pack of 2lbs of popcorn costs $8. What is the price of 9 lbs. of popcorn?

3.   If the price of 50 box units is $25 at Box Store. What is the price per 13 boxes?

4.   Amit checked the price of 100 yards of cloth at a mart which was list $45 for 100 yards. If he wants to buy 20 yards of cloth how much money, he has to pay?

5.   Julie bought a dozens of mangos for $4. If she wants to buy 18 more mangos, how much she has to pay more?

6.   At a pot outlet, 25 pots cost $250. If you have to only 8 pots, how much money you have to pay?

7.   At a dairy farm, farmer is selling 100 gallons of organic milk for $800. If Richa has to buy only 5 gallons of milk, how much money she has to pay to the farmer?

8.   Elton wants to a pair of shoes for himself, his brother and his cousin. If the price of 5 pair of shoes is $300. How much money does he need to buy pairs of shoes?

9.   Tom bought 20 donuts for breakfast on Tuesday, and paid $20. If Greg wants to buy a dozens of donuts, how much does he need?

10.   If a pack of 20 candies is sold for $12. Calculate the price for a dozens of candies?

11.   If there a sale at wholesale market "buy 2 pots and get 1 free" and price of 1 pot is $5. How much money you need to buy 3 pots?

12.   On Christmas, Grocery mart had a promotion if anyone would buy 2 drumsticks the he will get 2 drumsticks for free. If price of one drumstick is $1. How much will you pay for 12 drumsticks?

13.   On New Year Day, Amit bought few chocolates from Chocolate Parlor. If there is a promotion on new year to get 1 chocolate free with the purchase 2 chocolates. How much money do you need to buy 12 chocolates if the price of one chocolate is $2.5?

14.   If Coffee Shop is also running a promotion "Buy 1 Get 1 Free'. How much money does Lisa need to buy 3 donuts if the price of 1 donut is $1.5?

15. Price of a dozens of notebooks is listed as $12. How much money does Mike need to pay to buy 4 notebooks if there is a notebook free for every 2 notebooks purchase?

16.   There is BOGO deal, buy 2 boxes and get 2 boxes free. If 1 box is for $2, how much will it cost for 100 boxes?

17.   If price of 1 hat is $1.2, and there is a promotion 'Buy 1 Get 1' at wholesale store. You are planning to buy 200 for your retail store. How much money do you need?

18.   Buy 2 Kg of sugar and get 1 Kg of sugar free. Price of 1 Kg is $4. What is the price of 6 Kgs?

19.   If there a sale at wholesale market "buy 3 pots and get 1 free" and price of 1 pot is $10. How much money you need to buy 3 pots?

20.   On Christmas, Grocery mart had a promotion if anyone would buy 3 drumsticks the he will get 1 drumstick for free. If price of one drumstick is $1. How much will you pay for 12 drumsticks?

20.   CONVERT LENGTH AND HEIGHT UNITS

Convert each of the following lengths into corresponding units:

1. 9 Feet 8 Inches = _____ Inches
    a) 120 Inches
    b) 116 Inches

2. 41 Yards = _____ Feet
    a) 133 Feet
    b) 123 Feet

3. 12 Yards 3 Feet = _____ Feet
    a) 39 Feet
    b) 30 Feet

4. 3 Feet 5 Inches = _____ Inches
    a) 31 Inches
    b) 41 Inches

5. 139 Feet = _____ Yards _____ Inches
    a) 46 Yards 1 Feet
    b) 46 Yards 2 Feet

6. 86 Feet = _____ Yards _____ Feet
    a) 28 Yards 4 Feet
    b) 28 Yards 2 Feet

7. 12 Inches = _____ Feet
    a) 2 Feet
    b) 1 Feet

8. 236 Inches = _____ Feet _____ Inches
    a) 19 Feet 8 Inches
    b) 20 Feet 2 Inches

9. 21 Feet 2 Inches = _____ Inches
    a) 254 Inches
    b) 264 Inches

10. 66 Inches = _____ Feet _____ Inches
    a) 5 Feet 6 Inches
    b) 6 Feet 6 Inches

11. 150 Inches = _____ Feet _____ Inches
    a) 12 Feet 6 Inches
    b) 11 Feet 12 Inches

12. 31 Feet = _____ Yards _____ Feet
    a) 20 Yards 1 Inches
    b) 10 Yards 1 Feet

13. 72 Feet = _____ Yards _____ Feet
    a) 24 Yards 0 Feet
    b) 23 Yards 1 Feet

14. 3 Feet 1 Inches = _____ Inches
    a) 30 Inches
    b) 37 Inches

15. 110 Inches = ____ Feet ____ Inches
   a) 10 Feet 2 Inches
   b) 9 Feet 2 Inches

21. 22 Yards 2 Feet = ____ Feet
   a) 68 Feet
   b) 70 Feet

16. 162 Inches = ____ Feet ____ Inches
   a) 12 Feet 13 Inches
   b) 13 Feet 6 Inches

22. 8 Feet 5 Inches = ____ Inches
   a) 102 Inches
   b) 101 Inches

17. 144 Inches = ___ Feet ____ Inches
   a) 12 Feet 0 Inches
   b) 12 Feet 4 Inches

23. 22 Feet 1 Inches = ____ Inches
   a) 265 Inches
   b) 285 Inches

18. 72 Feet = ____ Yards ___ Feet
   a) 24 Yards 0 Feet
   b) 23 Yards 1 Feet

24. 241 Inches = ___ Feet ___ Inches
   a) 20 Feet 11 Inches
   b) 20 Feet 1 Inches

19. 16 Feet 8 Inches = ____ Inches
   a) 300 Inches
   b) 200 Inches

25. 40 Yards 2 Feet = ____ Feet
   a) 122 Feet
   b) 132 Feet

20. 140 Feet = ____ Yards ____ Inches
   a) 46 Yards 1 Feet
   b) 46 Yards 2 Feet

21.   CONVERT VOLUME UNITS

Choose the right conversion unit for each of the following volume unit:

1. 12 tablespoons =?
    a) 4 fluid ounces
    b) 6 fluid ounces

2. 4 gallons =?
    a) 16 quarts
    b) 24 quarts

3. 18 cups =?
    a) 1 pint
    b) 9 pints

4. 7 gallons =?
    a) 56 pints
    b) 72 pints

5. 5 quarts =?
    a) 20 pints
    b) 10 pints

6. 12 quarts =?
    a) 48 cups
    b) 56 cups

7. 16 quarts =?
    a) 8 gallons
    b) 4 gallons

8. 24 quarts =?
    a) 96 cups
    b) 108 cups

9. 2 pints =?
    a) 1 quart
    b) 4 quart

10. 36 teaspoons =?
    a) 6 tablespoons
    b) 12 tablespoons

11. 48 fluid ounces =?
    a) 12 cups
    b) 6 cups

12. 6 cups =?
    a) 48 fluid ounces
    b) 24 fluid ounces

13. 18 teaspoons =?
    a) 6 tablespoons
    b) 9 tablespoons

14. 48 quarts =?
    a) 208 cups
    b) 192 cups

15. 64 fluid ounces =?
   a) 8 pints
   b) 4 pints

16. 56 pints =?
   a) 14 gallons
   b) 7 gallons

17. 8 pints =?
   a) 1 gallons
   b) 2 gallons

18. 16 fluid ounces =?
   a) 2 pints
   b) 1 pints

19. 9 pints =?
   a) 18 cups
   b) 20 cups

20. 10 pints =?
   a) 5 quarts
   b) 10 quarts

21. 4 cups =?
   a) 2 quarts
   b) 1 quarts

22. 4 pints =?
   a) 64 fluid ounces
   b) 32 fluid ounces

23. 2 cups =?
   a) 1 pint
   b) 2 pints

24. 48 cups =?
   a) 12 quarts
   b) 24 quarts

25. 6 fluid ounces =?
   a) 18 tablespoons
   b) 12 tablespoons

22.   CONVERT WEIGHT UNITS

Choose the right conversion unit for each of the following weight unit:

1. 14,400 lb. = ___ tons ___ lb.
    a) 1 ton 4400 lb.
    b) 7 tons 400 lb.

2. 6, 800 lb. = ____ tons ____ lb.
    a) 3 tons 800 lb.
    b) 6 tons 800 lb.

3. 5 lb. 6 oz. = ____ oz.
    a) 86 oz.
    b) 96 oz.

4. 34 oz. = ____ lb. ___ oz.
    a) 2 lb. 3 oz.
    b) 2 lb. 2 oz.

5. 36,000 lb. = ____ tons ____ lb.
    a) 9 tons 0 lb.
    b) 18 tons 0 lb.

6. 9,200 lb. = ____ tons ____ lb.
    a) 4 tons 1200 lb.
    b) 9 tons 200 lb.

7. 10 lb. 6 oz. = ____ oz.
    a) 166 oz.
    b) 96 oz.

8. 9 tons 1600 lb. = _____ lb.
    a) 20,000 lb.
    b) 19,600 lb.

9. 36, 100 oz. = ____ tons ____ lb.
    a) 9 tons 100 lb.
    b) 18 tons 100 lb.

10. 7 tons 800 lb. = _____ lb.
    a) 7800 lb.
    b) 14, 800 lb.

11. 2 lb. 8 oz. = _____ oz.
    a) 40 oz.
    b) 32 oz.

12. 8,200 lb. = ____ tons ____ lb.
    a) 8 tons 200 lb.
    b) 4 tons 200 lb.

13. 1 ton 800 lb. = _____ lb.
    a) 2800 lb.
    b) 2000 lb.

14. 1 lb. 13 oz. = _____ oz.
    a) 30 oz.
    b) 29 oz.

15. 7 tons 300 lb. = _____ lb.
   a) 7300 lb.
   b) 14, 300 lb.

21. 50 oz. = ___ lb. ___oz.
   a) 3 lb. 2 oz.
   b) 4 lb. 2 oz.

16. 18, 200 oz. = _____ tons _____ lb.
   a) 9 tons 200 lb.
   b) 18 tons 200 lb.

22. 3 lb. 9 oz. = _____ oz.
   a) 60 oz.
   b) 57 oz.

17. 3 lb. 9 oz. = _____ oz.
   a) 56 oz.
   b) 60 oz.

23. 4 lb. 9 oz. = ___ oz.
   a) 70 oz.
   b) 73 oz.

18. 3 lb. 4 oz. = _____ oz.
   a) 34 oz.
   b) 52 oz.

24. 17 oz. = _____ lb. _____ oz.
   a) 1 lb. 1 oz.
   b) 2 lb. 1 oz.

19. 14,600 lb. = _____ tons _____ lb.
   a) 14 tons 600 lb.
   b) 7 tons 600 lb.

25. 18,000 lb. = _____tons _____ lb.
   a) 9 tons 0 lb.
   b) 18 tons 0 lb.

20. 4000 lb. = _____ tons _____ lb.
   a) 4 tons
   b) 2 tons

23. MEASUREMENT PROBLEMS (TRUE OR FALSE)

Verify whether each of the following conversion is correct (true) or not (false):

1. Is 2 Pints = 4 Quarts
   a) False
   b) True

2. Is 2 Cups = 4 Pint
   a) True
   b) False

3. Is 10 Pints = 1 Quarts
   a) True
   b) False

4. Is 10 Pints = 5 Quarts
   a) True
   b) False

5. Is 12 Tablespoons = 6 Fluid ounces
   a) False
   b) True

6. Is 16 Quarts = 4 Gallons
   a) False
   b) True

7. Is 9 Pints = 18 Cups
   a) True
   b) False

8. Is 4 Gallons = 16 Quarts
   a) True
   b) False

9. Is 48 Cups = 24 Quarts
   a) True
   b) False

10. Is 16 Quarts = 2 Gallons
    a) False
    b) True

11. Is 18 Teaspoons = 9 Tablespoons
    a) True
    b) False

12. Is 16 Fluid ounces = 8 Pint
    a) False
    b) True

13. Is   4 Gallons = 32 Quarts
    a) True
    b) False

14. Is 12 Tablespoons = 2 Fluid ounces
    a) False
    b) True

15. Is 2 Pints = 1 Quarts
    a) False
    b) True

16. Is 5 Quarts = 10 Pints
    a) False
    b) True

17. Is 18 Cups = 1 Pint
    a) True
    b) False

18. Is 18 Teaspoons = 6 Tablespoons
    a) True
    b) False

19. Is 2 Cups = 1 Pint
    a) True
    b) False

20. Is 48 Cups = 12 Quarts
    a) True
    b) False

21. Is 48 Fluid ounces = 12 Cups
    a) False
    b) True

22. Is 8 Pints = 4 Gallon
    a) True
    b) False

23. Is 64 Fluid ounces = 12 Pints
    a) False
    b) True

24. Is 4 Cups = 2 Quarts
    a) False
    b) True

25. Is 64 Fluid ounces = 4 Pints
    a) False
    b) True

26. Is 18 Cups = 6 Pint
    a) True
    b) False

27. Is 5 Quarts = 20 Pints
    a) False
    b) True

28. Is 4 Cups = 1 Quart
    a) False
    b) True

29. Is 16 Fluid ounces = 1 Pint
    a) False
    b) True

30. Is 56 Pints = 7 Gallons
    a) False
    b) True

31. Is 9 Pints = 24 Cups
    a) True
    b) False

32. Is 48 Fluid ounces = 6 Cups
    a) False
    b) True

33. Is 8 Pints = 1 Gallon
    a) True
    b) False

34. Is 56 Pints = 14 Gallons
    a) False
    b) True

24.   MEASURE LENGTH USING METRIC SYSTEM

Choose the right conversion unit for each of the following length using metric system:

1. 876123 mm. = _____ m.
    a) 876.123
    b) 87.6123

2. 9877865 mm. = _____ m.
    a) 987.7865
    b) 9877.865

3. 1.01 m.= _____ mm.
    a) 1010
    b) 10100

4. 20302mm. = _____ m.
    a) 20.302
    b) 203.02

5. 1000 mm. = _____ m.
    a) 1
    b) 2

6. 1.5 km. = _____ m.
    a) 1500
    b) 15000

7. 989889 cm.= _____ m.
    a) 98.9889
    b) 9898.89

8. .5 m.= _____ mm.
    a) 500
    b) 50

9. 5142 cm.= _____ m.
    a) 514.2
    b) 51.42

10. 12345 cm.= _____ m.
    a) 1234.5
    b) 123.45

11. 1 km. = _____ m.
    a) 1000
    b) 500

12. 10.12 km. = _____ m.
    a) 10120
    b) 101200

13. 9876780 cm.= _____ m.
    a) 9876.78
    b) 98767.8

14. 2.321 km. = _____ m.
    a) 2321
    b) 23210

15. 2.1 m.= _____ mm.
   a) 2100
   b) 21000

21. 1.2 km. = _____ m.
   a) 1200
   b) 12000

16. .01 m.= _____ mm.
   a) 10
   b) 100

22. 8971 cm.= _____ m.
   a) 8.971
   b) 89.71

17. 3.1 m.= _____ mm.
   a) 3100
   b) 310

23. 1 m.= _____ mm.
   a) 1000
   b) 500

18. 87654 cm.= _____ m.
   a) 87.654
   b) 876.54

24. 334433 mm. = _____ m.
   a) 334.433
   b) 33.4433

19. 980 cm.= _____ m.
   a) 98
   b) 9.8

25. 8176 mm. = _____ m.
   a) 8.176
   b) 81.76

20. 0.51 km. = _____ m.
   a) 510
   b) 501

25. MEASURE VOLUME USING METRIC SYSTEM

Choose the right conversion unit for each of the following volume using metric system:

1. 4242 cl. = _____ l.
   a) 4.242
   b) 42.42

2. 2.02 l.= _____ ml.
   a) 2020
   b) 20200

3. 7377364 ml. = _____ l.
   a) 737.7364
   b) 7377.364

4. 2 l.= _____ ml.
   a) 2000
   b) 400

5. 2.2 l. = _____ ml.
   a) 2200
   b) 22000

6. 3.2 l.= _____ ml.
   3200
   320

7. 20.22 l. = _____ ml.
   a) 20220
   b) 202200

8. 20302 ml. = _____ l.
   a) 20.302
   b) 203.02

9. 2000 ml. = _____ l.
   a) 2
   b) 20

10. 37644 cl. = _____ l.
    a) 37.644
    b) 376.44

11. 22344 cl. = _____ l.
    a) 22.344
    b) 223.44

12. 730 cl. = _____ l.
    a) 73
    b) 7.3

13. 7376730 cl. = _____ l.
    a) 737.673
    b) 73767.3

14. 2.2 l.= _____ ml.
    a) 2200
    b) 22000

15. 0.42 l. = _____ ml.
   a) 420
   b) 402

16. 2 l. = _____ ml.
   a) 2000
   b) 400

17. 0.02 l.= _____ ml.
   a) 20
   b) 200

18. 2.322 l. = _____ ml.
   a) 2322
   b) 23220

19. 3772 cl. = _____ l.
   a) 3.772
   b) 37.72

20. 0.4 l.= _____ ml.
   a) 400
   b) 40

21. 2.4 l. = _____ ml.
   a) 2400
   b) 24000

22. 376223 ml. = _____ l.
   a) 376.223
   b) 37.6223

23. 737337 cl. = _____ l.
   a) 73.7337
   b) 7373.37

24. 334433 ml. = _____ l.
   a) 334.433
   b) 33.4433

25. 3276 ml. = _____ l.
   a) 3.276
   b) 32.76

26.   MEASURE WEIGHT USING METRIC SYSTEM

Choose the right conversion unit for each of the following weight using metric system:

1. 60.62 kg. = _____ g.
    a) 60620
    b) 606200

2. 787887 g.= _____ kg.
    a) 78.7887
    b) 787.887

3. 0.5 tons = _____ kg.
    a) 500
    b) 50

4. 87654 g.= _____ kg.
    a) 876.54
    b) 87.654

5. 5642 g.= _____ kg.
    a) 56.42
    b) 5.642

6. 20502kg. = _____ tons
    a) 20.502
    b) 205.02

7. 6 tons = _____ kg.
    a) 6000
    b) 500

8. 554455 kg. = _____ tons
    a) 554.455
    b) 55.4455

9. 6 kg. = _____ g.
    a) 6000
    b) 500

10. 62545 g.= _____ kg.
    a) 625.45
    b) 62.545

11. 8776 g.= _____ kg.
    a) 87.76
    b) 8.776

12. 0.06 tons = _____ kg.
    a) 60
    b) 600

13. 7877865 kg. = _____ tons
    a) 787.7865
    b) 7877.865

14. 6000 kg. = _____ tons
    a) 6
    b) 2

15. 876625 kg. = _____ tons
   a) 876.625
   b) 87.6625

16. 5.6 tons = _____ kg.
   a) 5600
   b) 560

17. 2.526 kg. = _____ g.
   a) 2526
   b) 25260

18. 6.5 kg. = _____ g.
   a) 6500
   b) 65000

19. 8676 kg. = _____ tons
   a) 8.676
   b) 86.76

20. 2.6 tons = _____ kg.
   a) 2600
   b) 26000

21. 0.56 kg. = _____ g.
   560
   506

22. 6.2 kg. = _____ g.
   a) 6200
   b) 62000

23. 7876780 g.= _____ kg.
   a) 78767.8
   b) 7876.78

24. 6.06 tons = _____ kg.
   a) 6060
   b) 60600

25. 780 g.= _____ kg.
   a) 78
   b) 0.78

27.   MEASUREMENTS USING METRIC SYSTEM (TRUE OR FALSE)

Verify whether each of the following conversion is correct (true) or not (false):

1. Is 1.3 kg. = 1300 g
    a) True
    b) False

2. Is 87654 cl. = 87.654 l.
    a) True
    b) False

3. Is .01 kg. = 10 g.
    a) True
    b) False

4. Is 1.3 km.= 1300 m.
    a) True
    b) False

5. Is 8176 ml. = 8.176 l.
    a) True
    b) False

6. Is 1 km.= 1000 m.
    a) True
    b) False

7. Is 2.12 kg. = 2120 g.
    a) True
    b) False

8. Is 1 km.= 500 m.+ 300 m.+ 200 m.
    a) True
    b) False

9. Is 2.345 kg. = 2345 g.
    a) True
    b) False

10. Is 1 kg. + 500 g.= 1.5 kg.
    a) True
    b) False

11. Is 2.345 km.= 2345 m.
    a) True
    b) False

12. Is 0.01 km.= 10 m.
    a) True
    b) False

13. Is 989889 cl. = 9898.89 l.
    a) True
    b) False

14. Is 1 l. = 1000 ml.
    a) True
    b) False

15. Is 1 km.+ 500 m.= 1.5 km.
   a) True
   b) False

16. Is 9876780 cl. = 9876.780 l.
   a) True
   b) False

17. Is 2.12 km.= 2120 m.
   a) True
   b) False

18. Is 1 km. + 500 m.= 1500 m.
   a) True
   b) False

19. Is 1.2 l. = 1200 ml.
   a) True
   b) False

20. Is 1 km.+ 3 km.= 4000 m.
   a) True
   b) False

21. Is 1 kg. = 1000 g.
   a) True
   b) False

22. Is 1 kg. = 500 g.+ 300 g.+ 200 g.
   a) True
   b) False

23. Is 1 kg. + 500 g.= 1500 g.
   a) True
   b) False

24. Is 1 kg. + 3 kg. = 4000 g.
   a) True
   b) False

28. CONVERSION OF TIME UNITS (HOURS, MINUTES AND SECONDS)

Fill in the blanks with right converted unit.

1. 480 Minutes = _____ Hours

2. 240 Minutes = _____ Hours

3. True or False:
   8 Minutes = 420 Seconds
   a) False
   b) True

4. 8 Hours = _____ Minutes
   a) 480
   b) 420
   c) 540
   d) 450

5. True or False:
   7 Minutes = 420 Seconds
   a) True
   b) False

6. 3 Hours = _____ Minutes

7. 420 Minutes = _____ Hours

8. 10 Minutes = _____ Seconds

9. How many minutes are in a day?

10. 9 Minutes = _____ Seconds
    a) 540
    b) 480

11. How many minutes are in an hour?

12. 360 Minutes = _____ Hours

13. 300 Minutes = _____ Hours
    a) 5
    b) 4
    c) 6
    d) 3

14. 300 Minutes = _____ Hours

15. True or False:
    6 Hours = 300 Minutes
    a) False
    b) True

16. True or False:
    420 Minutes = 7 Hours
    a) True
    b) False

17. 6 Hours = ____ Minutes

18. 300 Seconds = ____ Minutes

19. True or False:
   5 Hours = 300 Minutes
   a) True
   b) False

20. 5 Hours = ____ Minutes

21. True or False:
   480 Minutes = 7 Hours
   a) False
   b) True

22. How many seconds are in a minute?

23. 8 Minutes = ____ Seconds

24. How many hours are in a day?

25. 2 Hours = ____ Minutes

26. 360 Minutes = ____ Hours
   a) 6
   b) 5
   c) 7
   d) 4

27. 6 Minutes = ____ Seconds

28. 240 Seconds = ____ Minutes

29. 420 Seconds = ____ Minutes

30. 5 Minutes = ____ Seconds
   a) 300
   b) 240
   c) 360
   d) 270

31. 4 Hours = ____ Minutes

32. 7 Hours = ____ Minutes
   a) 420
   b) 360
   c) 480
   d) 390

29. CONVERSION OF TIME USING MULTIPLE TIME UNITS

Fill in the blanks with right converted unit:

1. 3 Weeks 2 Days =____ Days

2. 4 Weeks 3 Days =____ Days

3. ____ Minutes 15 Seconds =1335 Seconds

4. 8 Minutes 18 Seconds =____ Seconds

5. ____Days 3 Hours =147 Hours

6. ____Days 5 Hours =101 Hours

7. 8 Weeks ___Days =58 Days

8. ____Days 2 Hours =122 Hours

9. 5 Hours 20 Minutes =____ Minutes

10. ____ Hours 18 Minutes =198 Minutes

11. 2 Weeks ___Days =19 Days

12. ___Weeks 5 Days =33 Days

13. ___ Minutes 20 Seconds =500 Seconds

14. ___Days 2 Hours =170 Hours

15. 6 Hours 17 Minutes =____ Minutes

16. 7 Hours ___Minutes =450 Minutes

17. 5 Minutes 15 Seconds =____ Seconds

18. 8 Minutes ___Seconds=510 Seconds

19. ____ Hours 25 Minutes=385 Minutes

20. ___Weeks 3 Days =45 Days

21. 8 Days ___Hours =194 Hours

22. ____ Hours 30 Minutes =330 Minutes

23. 3 Days 2 Hours =____ Hours

24. ___Minutes 35 Seconds =755 Seconds

25. 5 Weeks ___Days =37 Days

26. 2 Days ___Hours =53 Hours

27. 6 Weeks ___Days =44 Days

28. ___Minutes 46 Seconds =766 Seconds

29. 15 Minutes ___Seconds =915 Seconds

30. 6 Days ___Hours =146 Hours

31. ___Days 2 Hours =74 Hours

32. ____ Hours 15 Minutes =435 Minutes

33. 5 Days 2 Hours =____ Hours

34. 8 Hours ___Minutes =495 Minutes

35. 2 Hours ___Minutes =156 Minutes

36. 4 Days 3 Hours =____ Hours

37. 3 Hours 34 Minutes =____ Minutes

38. 4 Hours 15 Minutes =____ Minutes

39. 4 Hours 35 Minutes =____ Minutes

40. 10 Minutes 30 Seconds =____ Seconds

30.   TIME PROBLEMS (TRUE OR FALSE)

Check whether following conversions are true or false:

1.   8 Days 2 Hours =218 Hours
   a) False
   b) True

8.   4 Hours 15 Minutes =255 Minutes
   a) True
   b) False

2.   3 Days 2 Hours =74 Hours
   a) True
   b) False

9.   5 Days 2 Hours =122 Hours
   a) True
   b) False

3. 12 Minutes 46 Seconds =766 Seconds
   a) True
   b) False

10. 3 Hours 34 Minutes =274 Minutes
   a) False
   b) True

4.   2 Weeks 5 Days =19 Days
   a) True
   b) False

11. 5 Hours 30 Minutes =270 Minutes
   a) False
   b) True

5.   6 Weeks 3 Days =45 Days
   a) True
   b) False

12.   5 Weeks 2 Days =30 Days
   a) False
   b) True

6.   6 Hours 25 Minutes =385 Minutes
   a) True
   b) False

13. 3 Hours 34 Minutes =214 Minutes
   a) True
   b) False

7. 4 Minutes 25 Seconds =325 Seconds
   a) False
   b) True

14. 3 Hours 18 Minutes =198 Minutes
   a) True
   b) False

15. 7 Minutes 15 Seconds =435 Seconds
   a) True
   b) False

23.   5 Hours 20 Minutes =320 Minutes
   a) True
   b) False

16. 22 Minutes 15 Seconds=1335 Seconds
   a) True
   b) False

24. 12 Minutes 25 Seconds =805 Seconds
   a) False
   b) True

17.   5 Weeks 2 Days =44 Days
   a) False
   b) True

25.   2 Weeks 2 Days =23 Days
   a) False
   b) True

18.   7 Days 3 Hours =195 Hours
   a) False
   b) True

26.   2 Days 5 Hours =53 Hours
   a) True
   b) False

19.   4 Days 5 Hours =101 Hours
   a) True
   b) False

27.20 Minutes 15 Seconds =1215 Seconds
   a) True
   b) False

20. 12 Minutes 35 Seconds =755 Seconds
   a) True
   b) False

28.   4 Minutes 25 Seconds =265 Seconds
   a) True
   b) False

21.   5 Weeks 2 Days =44 Days
   a) False
   b) True

29.   4 Days 5 Hours =77 Hours
   a) False
   b) True

22.   6 Weeks 5 Days =47 Days
   a) True
   b) False

30. 20 Minutes 15 Seconds=1275 Seconds
   a) False
   b) True

31. 4 Weeks 5 Days =33 Days
   a) True
   b) False

32. 7 Hours 30 Minutes =510 Minutes
   a) False
   b) True

33. 5 Minutes 15 Seconds =375 Seconds
   a) False
   b) True

34. 22 Minutes 15 Seconds=1275 Seconds
   a) False
   b) True

35. 7 Weeks 3 Days =59 Days
   a) False
   b) True

36. 6 Days 5 Hours =149 Hours
   a) True
   b) False

37. 3 Days 2 Hours =74 Hours
   a) True
   b) False

38. 8 Minutes 18 Seconds=558 Seconds
   a) False
   b) True

39. 8 Weeks 2 Days =65 Days
   a) False
   b) True

40. 8 Weeks 2 Days =58 Days
   a) True
   b) False

31.   UNDERSTAND TIME SCHEDULE

1.   Mike always has busy Saturday as he goes in number of classes.
   1) Swimming starts at 9:15 AM and ends at 9:50 AM
   2) Piano class starts at 11:15 AM and ends at 11:45 AM
   3) Lunch is always planned between 12:00 PM to 12:30 PM
   4) Then he goes to play soccer from 12:30 PM to 1:45 PM

How long does he play soccer?
   a) 1 H :15 M
   b) 2 H :15 M
   c) 1 H
   d) 15 M

2.   A train runs between Fremont and San Francisco every day. Train schedule looks like as follows:
   1) Fremont   8:20 AM
   2) Union City   8:27 AM
   3) Bay Fair   8:37 AM
   4) San Leandro   8:49 AM
   5) Oakland   8:59 AM
   6) Civic Center   9:05 AM
   7) San Francisco   9:10 AM

How much time does it take between Oakland and Civic Center?
   a) 6 Minutes
   b) 5 Minutes
   c) 16 Minutes
   d) 60 Minutes

3.   Tomorrow is World's Badminton Championship final:
   1) Women's Final between 10:30 AM and 11:30 AM
   2) Women Double's Final between 11:45 AM and 12:45 PM
   3) Mixed Double's Final between 1:00 PM and 1:15 PM
   4) Men Double's Final between 1:30 PM and 2:30 PM
   5) Men's Final between 2:45 PM and 3:45 PM
   6) Award Ceremony between 4:00 PM and 4:30 PM

How much time is between Men Double's and Men's finals?

4. There are 4 meetings planned on the first day of school.
    1) Coffee with principal starts at 7:15 AM and ends at 8:15 AM
    2) School's tour with principal starts at 8:30 AM and ends at 9:15 AM
    3) Parents and Class Teacher meeting starts at 9:30 AM and ends at 10:30AM
    4) Students induction starts at XX:YY AM and ends at 11:30 AM

If Students induction is planned after 10 Minutes of Parents Teacher meeting. What time does students induction start?
    a) 10:40:00 AM
    b) 10:35:00 AM
    c) 10:45:00 AM
    d) 10:30:00 AM

5. There are number of shows and events running at Central Theme Park in the summer:
    1) Big Man's show between 11:25 AM and 11:55 AM
    2) Monkey Show between 12:30 PM and 12:55 PM
    3) Animals 3D movie between 1:15 PM and 1:55 PM
    4) Fish Feeding between 2:00 PM and 2:30 PM
    5) Birds show between 3:00 PM and 3:40 PM

Which event starts after Animals 3D movie?
    a) Fish Feeding
    b) Birds show
    c) Monkey Show
    d) Big Man's show

6. There are number of events planned on school's annual day program as follows:
    1) Women's basketball between 1:30 PM to 2:30 PM
    2) Men's basketball between 2:45 PM to 3:45 PM
    3) School's Band Performance between 4:00 PM and 4:45 PM
    4) Dance Performance between 4:45 PM to 6:00 PM
    5) Award Ceremony between 6:00 PM and 6:30 PM

How long is the band performance?

7. A train runs between Fremont and San Francisco every day. Train schedule shows both arrival and departure times as follows:
    1) Fremont   8:20 AM   8:22 AM
    2) Union City   8:29 AM   8:31 AM
    3) Bay Fair   8:39 AM   8:41 AM
    4) San Leandro   8:49 AM   8:51 AM
    5) Oakland   9:03 AM   9:08 AM
    6) Civic Center   9:15 AM   9:17 AM
    7) San Francisco 9:20 AM

How long is the stop over at Oakland?
    a) 5 Minutes
    b) 2 Minutes
    c) 3 Minutes
    d) 12 Minutes

8. There are 4 meetings planned on the first day of school.
    1) Coffee with the principal starts at 7:15 AM and ends at 8:15 AM
    2) School's tour with the principal starts at 8:30 AM and ends at 9:15 AM
    3) Parents and Class Teacher meeting starts at 9:30 AM and ends at 10:30 AM
    4) Students induction starts at 10:45 AM and ends at 11:30 AM

Which event ends at 9:15 AM?
    a) School's tour with the principal
    b) Coffee with the principal
    c) Parents and Class Teacher meeting
    d) Students induction

9. 3rd Grade's class schedule is as follows:
    1) Attendance and review of last day work between 8:25 AM and 8:45 AM
    2) Mathematics between 8:45 AM to 9:30 AM
    3) Music between 9:30 AM and 10:30 AM
    4) Science between 10:30 AM to 11:30 AM
    5) Lunch Break between 11:30 AM to 12:30 AM
    6) English between 12:30 AM to 1:15 PM

What event or class ends at 11:30 AM?
    a) Science   b) Mathematics   c) Lunch Break   d) English

10. Tomorrow is World's Badminton Championship final:
     1) Women's Final between 10:30 AM and 11:30 AM
     2) Women Double's Final between 11:45 AM and 12:45 PM
     3) Mixed Double's Final between 1:00 PM and 1:15 PM
     4) Men Double's Final between 1:30 PM and 2:30 PM
     5) Men's Final between 2:45 PM and 3:45 PM
     6) Award Ceremony between 4:00 PM and 4:30 PM

How much gap is between any 2 events?
     a) 15 Minutes
     b) 30 Minutes
     c) 20 Minutes
     d) 25 Minutes

11. 3rd Grade's class schedule is as follows:
     1) Attendance and review of last day work between 8:25 AM and 8:45 AM
     2) Mathematics between 8:45 AM to 9:30 AM
     3) Music between 9:30 AM and 10:30 AM
     4) Science between 10:30 AM to 11:30 AM
     5) Lunch Break between 11:30 AM to 12:30 AM
     6) English between 12:30 AM to 1:15 PM

What event or class starts at 11:30 AM?
     a) Lunch Break
     b) Mathematics
     c) Science
     d) English

12. Tomorrow is World's Badminton Championship final:
   1) Women's Final between 10:30 AM and 11:30 AM
   2) Women Double's Final between XX:YY AM and 12:45 PM
   3) Mixed Double's Final between 1:00 PM and 1:15 PM
   4) Men Double's Final between 1:30 PM and 2:30 PM
   5) Men's Final between 2:45 PM and 3:45 PM
   6) Award Ceremony between 4:00 PM and 4:30 PM

If Women Double's Final is planned after 25 Minutes of Women's Final. What time will Women Double's Final start?
   a) 11:55:00 AM
   b) 12:00:00 PM
   c) 11:45:00 AM
   d) 11:40:00 AM

13. Tomorrow is World's Badminton Championship final:
   1) Women's Final between 10:30 AM and 11:30 AM
   2) Women Double's Final between XX:YY AM and 12:45 PM
   3) Mixed Double's Final between 1:00 PM and 1:15 PM
   4) Men Double's Final between 1:30 PM and 2:30 PM
   5) Men's Final between 2:45 PM and 3:45 PM
   6) Award Ceremony between 4:00 PM and 4:30 PM

If Women Double's Final is planned after 20 Minutes of Women's Final. What time will Women Double's Final start?
   a) 11:50:00 AM
   b) 12:00:00 PM
   c) 11:45:00 AM
   d) 11:55:00 AM

14. There are 4 meetings planned on the first day of school.
    1) Coffee with the principal starts at 7:15 AM and ends at 8:15 AM
    2) School's tour with the principal starts at 8:30 AM and ends at 9:15 AM
    3) Parents and Class Teacher meeting starts at 9:30 AM and ends at 10:30 AM
    4) Students induction starts at 10:45 AM and ends at 11:30 AM

Which is the last event on first day of the school?
    a) Students induction
    b) Coffee with the principal
    c) Parents and Class Teacher meeting
    d) School's tour with the principal

15. A train runs between Fremont and San Francisco every day. Train schedule shows both arrival and departure times as follows:

    1) Fremont   8:20 AM   8:22 AM
    2) Union City   8:29 AM   8:31 AM
    3) Bay Fair   8:39 AM   8:41 AM
    4) San Leandro   8:49 AM   8:51 AM
    5) Oakland   8:59 AM   9:05 AM
    6) Civic Center   9:15 AM   9:17 AM
    7) San Francisco 9:20 AM

How long is the stop over at Oakland?
    a) 6 Minutes
    b) 5 Minutes
    c) 3 Minutes
    d) 12 Minutes

16.   There are number of shows and events running at Central Theme Park in the summer:
     1) Big Man's show between 11:25 AM and 11:55 AM
     2) Monkey Show between 12:30 PM and 12:55 PM
     3) Animals 3D movie between 1:15 PM and 1:55 PM
     4) Fish Feeding between 2:00 PM and 2:30 PM
     5) Birds show between 3:00 PM and 3:40 PM

Which event is before Animals 3D movie?
    a) Monkey Show
    b) Birds show
    c) Fish Feeding
    d) Big Man's show

17.   There are 4 meetings planned on the first day of school.
     1) Coffee with principal starts at 7:15 AM and ends at 8:15 AM
     2) School's tour with principal starts at 8:30 AM and ends at 9:15 AM
     3) Parents and Class Teacher meeting starts at 9:30 AM and ends at XX: YY AM
     4) Students induction starts at 10:45 AM and ends at 11:30 AM

If Parents and Class Teacher ends 10 Minutes before Students induction starts. What time does Parents and Class Teacher meeting end?
    a) 10:35:00 AM
    b) 10:40:00 AM
    c) 10:45:00 AM
    d) 10:30:00 AM

18. There are number of events planned on school's annual day program as follows:
   1) Women's basketball between 1:30 PM to 2:30 PM
   2) Men's basketball between 2:45 PM to 3:45 PM
   3) School's Band Performance between 4:00 PM and 4:45 PM
   4) Dance Performance between 4:45 PM to 6:00 PM
   5) Award Ceremony between 6:00 PM and 6:30 PM

How long is the award ceremony?
   a) 30 Minutes
   b) 55 Minutes
   c) 40 Minutes
   d) 35 Minutes

19. A train runs between Fremont and San Francisco every day. Train schedule looks like as follows:
   1) Fremont   8:20 AM
   2) Union City   8:27 AM
   3) Bay Fair   8:37 AM
   4) San Leandro   8:49 AM
   5) Oakland   8:59 AM
   6) Civic Center   9:05 AM
   7) San Francisco   9:10 AM

How much time does it take between Bay Fair and San Leandro?
   a) 12 Minutes
   b) 14 Minutes
   c) 15 Minutes
   d) 13 Minutes

20. Mike always has busy Saturday as he goes in number of classes.
    1) Swimming starts at 9:15 AM and ends at 9:50 AM
    2) Piano class starts at 11:15 AM and ends at 11:45 AM
    3) Lunch is always planned between 12:00 PM to 12:30 PM
    4) Then he goes to play soccer from 12:30 PM to 1:45 PM

How long does he plan for lunch?
    a) 30 Minutes
    b) 45 Minutes
    c) 35 Minutes
    d) 25 Minutes

32.   TIME WORD PROBLEMS (ELAPSED TIME, START TIME AND END TIME)

1.   If the current time is 3:25. What time will it be after 1 hour 15 minutes? Write your answer in time format HH:MM (ex 5:45).

2.   If the current time is 7:15. What time will it be after 1 hour 30 minutes? Write your answer in time format HH:MM (ex 5:45).

3.   Charlie started to his work at 8:15 A.M. There was lot of traffic on the road so he reached office at 9:40 A.M. How much time did he take to reach office? Write your answer in time format HH:MM (ex 5:45).

4.   If the current time is 2:15. What time was it before 1 hour 15 minutes? Write your answer in time format HH:MM (ex 5:45).

5.   Mr. Alvin goes to gym every day. He started exercise at 8:25 A.M. today. He exercised for almost 1 hour 35 minutes. What time did he finish exercising? Write your answer in time format HH:MM (ex 5:45).

6.   Ramona went to a movie theater to watch a movie. Movie started at 6:25 P.M. and finished at 8:50 P.M. How long was the movie? Write your answer in time format HH:MM (ex 5:45).

7.   If the current time is 9:15. What time will it be after 1 hour 45 minutes? Write your answer in time format HH:MM (ex 5:45).

8.   Joe and his dad started playing tennis at 11:30 A.M. They took some rest after sometime and started again. By the time, they finished playing it was 1:15 P.M. How long did they play? Write your answer in time format HH:MM (ex 5:45).

9. Emily went for shopping at 11:20 A.M. on Sunday. She came back home at 2:05 P.M. How long did she take to finish her shopping? Write your answer in time format HH:MM (ex 5:45).

10. It is half past 5 right now. What time will it be after 2 hours 15 minutes? Write your answer in time format HH:MM (ex 5:45).

11. If the current time is 8:15. What time was it before 1 hour 30 minutes? Write your answer in time format HH:MM (ex 5:45).

12. On Sunday, Shawn took shower at 10:30 A.M. By the time, he got ready it was 11:35 A.M. How long did he take to get ready? Write your answer in time format HH:MM (ex 5:45).

13. There was a dance party at school which started at 7:15 P.M. and finished at 9:45 P.M. How long did the dance party continue? Write your answer in time format HH:MM (ex 5:45).

14. It is quarter past 5 right now. What time was it before 1 hour? Write your answer in time format HH:MM (ex 5:45).

15. It is half past 3 right now. What time was it before 1 hour 30 minutes? Write your answer in time format HH:MM (ex 5:45).

16. Michelle's mom started cooking dinner at 6:45 P.M. and she finished cooking at 8:05. How long did she take to cook the dinner? Write your answer in time format HH:MM (ex 5:45).

17. Michael woke up at 6:30 A.M. He started to go to school at 8:00 A.M. How long did he take to get ready for the school? Write your answer in time format HH:MM (ex 5:45).

18. It is quarter past 4 right now. What time will it be after 2 hours? Write your answer in time format HH:MM (ex 5:45).

19. If the current time is 9:30. What time was it be before 1 hour 30 minutes? Write your answer in time format HH:MM (ex 5:45).

20. She started cleaning at 9:25 A.M. today. She cleaned for almost 1 hour 45 minutes. What time did she finish cleaning? Write your answer in time format HH:MM (ex 5:45).

33.   AVERAGE, MEAN, MEDIAN

1.   What is the average of
10, 20, 30, 20, 20

2.   What is the mean of
11, 22, 33

3.   What is the median of
11, 22, 33, 16, 16, 17, 18

4.   What is the average of
4, 8, 12

5.   What is the average of
5, 10, 15, 10

6.   What is the average of
12, 24, 12, 16

7.   What is the median of
9, 18, 27, 10, 11, 12, 5

8.   What is the mean of
4, 12, 20, 8, 6

9.   What is the average of
8, 12, 16, 12, 12, 12

10.   What is the median of
10, 10, 40, 20, 20

11.   What is the average of
5, 10, 15, 10, 10

12.   What is the average of
12, 24, 12

13.   What is the average of
5, 5, 20, 10

14.   What is the mean of
7, 21, 35, 45

15.   What is the median of
3, 6, 9, 4, 8

16.   What is the median of
6, 12, 18, 12, 12

17.   What is the mean of
6, 12, 18, 12, 12, 12

18.   What is the mean of
5, 10, 30, 6, 4

19. What is the median of
15, 25, 35, 12, 12, 3, 12

20. What is the average of
7, 14, 21, 14, 14, 14

21. What is the mean of
3, 6, 9, 6

22. What is the median of
7, 21, 35

23. What is the average of
12, 12, 12, 12, 12

24. What is the mean of
6, 12, 18, 12, 12

25. What is the average of
3, 6, 9

26. What is the average of
7, 14, 21

27. What is the mean of
5, 10, 30

28. What is the average of
5, 5, 20, 10, 10

29. What is the average of 12, 24, 12,
16, 16

30. What is the median of
7, 21, 35, 10, 10, 25, 35

31. What is the mean of
15, 25, 35, 12, 12, 3

32. What is the mean of
10, 10, 40, 20, 20, 140

33. What is the average of
3, 6, 9, 6, 6, 6

34. What is the mean of
8, 8, 32, 14, 14, 14

35. What is the median of
8, 8, 32, 14, 8

36. What is the median of
8, 8, 32, 14, 14, 14, 14

37. What is the mean of
15, 25, 35

38. What is the mean of
11, 22, 33, 11, 33

39. What is the mean of
3, 6, 9

40. What is the mean of
4, 12, 20, 8

34.   MODE AND RANGE

1.   What is the mode of
7, 7, 35

2.   What is the range of
16, 8, 32, 8

3.   What is the mode of
10, 10, 40, 10, 40

4.   What is the mode of
9, 18, 27, 19, 27

5.   What is the mode of
5, 30, 30

6.   What is the mode of
3, 6, 9, 4, 9, 28, 9

7.   What is the mode of
10, 20, 40, 20, 20, 14, 20

8.   What is the range of
10, 10, 40, 20, 50, 30

9.   What is the range of
8, 12, 20, 4

10. What is the range of
3, 6, 9

11. What is the range of
12, 6, 18, 12, 72, 12

12. What is the mode of
3, 6, 3

13. What is the range of
10, 18, 27, 9

14. What is the mode of
8, 18, 32, 14, 32

15. What is the range of
22, 22, 33, 11

16. What is the range of
4, 12, 20

17. What is the range of
5, 10, 30

18. What is the range of
15, 10, 30, 5

19. What is the range of
15, 25, 45, 15, 50, 35

20. What is the mode of
33, 22, 33, 11, 33

21. What is the range of
4, 10, 30, 6, 5, 30

22. What is the range of
22, 11, 33, 16, 39, 16

23. What is the range of
12, 4, 20, 8, 56, 48

24. What is the range of
21, 7, 35, 10, 41, 25

25. What is the range of
25, 25, 35, 15

26. What is the mode of
11, 22, 33, 16, 16, 17, 18

27. What is the range of
20, 10, 40, 10

28. What is the mode of
3, 6, 9, 4, 9

29. What is the range of
10, 10, 40

30. What is the mode of
15, 25, 35, 35, 35

31. What is the range of
12, 12, 18, 6

32. What is the range of
25, 3, 35, 12, 36, 15

33. What is the mode of
6, 12, 18, 12, 12, 12, 18

34. What is the range of
6, 12, 18, 12, 12, 18

35. What is the mode of
15, 25, 35, 12, 12, 3, 12

36. What is the mode of
9, 18, 27, 10, 11, 27, 27

37. What is the range of
11, 22, 33

38. What is the range of
10, 10, 40, 20, 20, 40

39. What is the range of
8, 8, 32

40. What is the mode of
6, 6, 18

35. AVERAGE, MEAN, MEDIAN, MODE AND RANGE (TRUE OR FALSE)

Verify whether each of the following statement is correct (true) or not (false).

1. The average of 2, 4, 6 is 4
    a) True
    b) False

2. The mode of 7, 21, 35, 10, 35 is 35
    a) True
    b) False

3. The mode of 5, 30, 30 is 30
    a) True
    b) False

4. The range of 4, 12, 20 is 16
    a) True
    b) False

5. The mean of 7, 21, 35, 45 is 27
    a) True
    b) False

6. The range of 9, 18, 27 is 27
    a) False
    b) True

7. The average of 12, 12, 12 is 14
    a) False
    b) True

8. The range of 11, 22, 33 is 33
    a) False
    b) True

9. The mean of 7, 21, 35 is 21
    a) True
    b) False

10. The median of 25, 35, 15 is 35
    a) False
    b) True

11. The range of 10, 10, 40 is 40
    a) False
    b) True

12. The average of 8, 12, 16 is 12
    a) True
    b) False

13. The average of 5, 10, 15 is 10
    a) True
    b) False

14. The median of 4, 12, 20, 8, 6 is 8
    a) True
    b) False

15. The mode of 6, 12, 18, 18, 18 is 18
    a) True
    b) False

16. The range of 6, 12, 18 is 12
    a) True
    b) False

17. The mode of 9, 18, 27, 19, 27 is 9
    a) False
    b) True

18. The median of 10, 10, 40, 20, 20 is 30
    a) False
    b) True

19. The range of 15, 25, 35 is 35
    a) False
    b) True

20. The mean of 15, 25, 35 is 23
    a) False
    b) True

21. The mean of 6, 12, 18, 12 is 12
    a) True
    b) False

22. The range of 35, 21, 45, 7 is 38
    a) True
    b) False

23. The median of 15, 25, 35, 15, 50 is 20
    False
    True

24. The range of 20, 10, 40, 10 is 40
    a) False
    b) True

25. The mode of 18, 9, 18 is 9
    a) False
    b) True

26. The mean of 3, 6, 9 is 6
    a) True
    b) False

27. The mean of 9, 18, 27 is 16
    a) False
    b) True

28. The median of 5, 10, 30, 6, 4 is 6
    a) True
    b) False

29. The median of 8, 32, 8 is 32
    a) False
    b) True

30. The mean of 6, 12, 18 is 12
    a) True
    b) False

31. The average of 12, 12, 12, 12 is 15
   a) False
   b) True

32. The mode of 15, 25, 35, 35, 35 is 25
   a) False
   b) True

33. The mean of 8, 8, 32 is 14
   a) False
   b) True

34. The median of 6, 12, 18, 12, 12 is 12
   a) True
   b) False

35. The mean of 10, 10, 40, 20 is 19
   a) False
   b) True

36. The mode of 22, 11, 11 is 22
   a) False
   b) True

37. The mode of 25, 15, 15 is 25
   a) False
   b) True

38. The median of 5, 10, 30 is 10
   a) True
   b) False

39. The mean of 9, 18, 27, 10 is 15
   a) False
   b) True

40. The mean of 5, 10, 30 is 15
   a) True
   b) False

36.   AVERAGE, MEAN, MEDIAN, MODE AND RANGE (WORD PROBLEMS)

1.   Sheila made number of cupcakes with different flavored on Christmas. She made 3 chocolates, 6 vanillas, 9 banana flavored, 6 strawberry flavored, 6 regular. What is the average number of cupcakes of each flavor, she made?

2.   There are number of books in public library. There are 22 Hindi, 22 English, 33 Social Studies and 11 History books. What is the range of given number of books?

3.   There are number of fruits in the fruit section at grocery store. There 18 apples, 18 oranges, 9 pineapples. What is the value of mode for given number of fruits?

4.   Sheila made number of cupcakes with different flavored on Christmas. She made 3 chocolates, 6 vanillas, 9 banana flavored, 6 strawberry flavored, 6 regular. What is the average number of cupcakes of each flavor, she made?

5.   There are number of fruits in the fruit section at grocery store. There 22 apples, 11 oranges, 33 pineapples. What is the median value?

6.   Steve has number of books in his home library. He has 2 Hindi, 4 English, 6 Science, 4 History, and 4 Social Studies books. What is the average number of books of each subject in his library?

7.   There are 4 blue pencils, 12 red pencils, 20 yellow pencils, 8 black pencils, 6 purple pencils and 20 green pencils in a box. What is the range of given number of pencils?

8.   There are number of cupcakes in the bakery. There are 3 chocolates, 6 vanillas,9 strawberry flavored, 4 banana flavored, 8 orange flavored and 9 regular one. What is the range of given number of cupcakes?

9.   There are 4 blue pencils, 12 red pencils, 20 yellow pencils, 8 black pencils, 6 purple pencils and 20 green pencils in a box. What is the range of given number of pencils?

10.   Paul has number of fruits in his basket. He has 4 apples, 8 oranges, 12 pineapples, 8 bananas, 8 mangos. What is the average number of fruit of each kind in his basket?

11.   There are number of fruits in the fruit section at grocery store. There 11 apples, 22 oranges, 33 pineapples, 11 bananas, 33 mangos. What is the mean of fruits of each kind?

12.   There are number of fruits in the fruit section at grocery store. There 10 apples, 18 oranges, 27 pineapples, and 9 mangos. What is the range of given number of fruits?

13.   There are number of cupcakes in the bakery. There are 18 chocolates, 9 vanillas and 27 regular one. What is the median value?

14.   There are 8 blue pencils, 12 red pencils, 16 yellow pencils, and 12 purple pencils in a box. What is the average number of pencils of each color in the box?

15.   There are number of fruits in the fruit section at grocery store. There 11 apples, 22 oranges, 33 pineapples, 11 bananas, 33 mangos. What is the mean of fruits of each kind?

16.   There are number of fruits in the fruit section at grocery store. There 18 apples, 18 oranges, 9 pineapples. What is the value of mode for given number of fruits?

17. There are 5 red marbles, 10 blue marbles, 15 yellow marbles and 10 green marbles on the ground. What is the average number of marbles of each color on the ground?

18. There are 3 blue pencils, 6 red pencils, 9 yellow pencils, 4 black pencils, and 4 green pencils in a box. What is the median value?

19. There are number of cupcakes in the bakery. There are 3 chocolates, 6 vanillas, 9 banana flavored, 4 strawberry flavored and 9 regular one. What is the value of mode for given number of cupcakes?

20. Steve has number of books in his home library. He has 2 Hindi, 4 English, 6 Science, 4 History, and 4 Social Studies books. What is the average number of books of each subject in his library?

21. There are 4 blue pencils, 12 red pencils, 20 yellow pencils, 8 black pencils, and 20 green pencils in a box. What is the value of mode for given number of pencils?

22. There are 5 red marbles, 10 blue marbles, 30 yellow marbles, 6 black marbles, and 30 green marbles on the ground. What is the value of mode for given number of marbles?

23. There are 4 red marbles, 10 blue marbles, 30 yellow marbles, 6 black marbles, 5 purple marbles and 30 green marbles on the ground. What is the range of given number of marbles?

24. There are number of books in public library. There are 25 Hindi, 15 English and 35 Social Studies books. What is the median value?

25. There are 3 blue pencils, 6 red pencils, 9 yellow pencils, 4 black pencils, and 4 green pencils in a box. What is the median value?

26. There are number of books in public library. There are 22 Hindi, 11 English and 11 Social Studies books. What is the value of mode for given number of books?

27. There are number of cupcakes in the bakery. There are 3 chocolates, 6 vanillas,9 strawberry flavored, 4 banana flavored, 8 orange flavored and 9 regular one. What is the range of given number of cupcakes?

28. There are number of books in public library. There are 15 Hindi, 25 English, 35 Science, 15 History, and 50 Social Studies books. What is the mean of books of each subject?

29. There are number of cupcakes in the bakery. There are 3 chocolates, 6 vanillas, 9 banana flavored, 4 strawberry flavored and 9 regular one. What is the value of mode for given number of cupcakes?

30. There are number of cupcakes in the bakery. There are 18 chocolates, 9 vanillas and 27 regular one. What is the median value?

31. There are 4 red marbles, 12 blue marbles, 20 yellow marbles, 8 black marbles, and 6 green marbles on the ground. What is the median value?

32. There are 4 red marbles, 12 blue marbles, 20 yellow marbles, 8 black marbles, 8 purple marbles and 56 green marbles on the ground. What is the mean of marbles of each color?

33. There are number of books in public library. There are 22 Hindi, 11 English and 11 Social Studies books. What is the value of mode for given number of books?

34. There are 4 red marbles, 12 blue marbles, 20 yellow marbles, 8 black marbles, 8 purple marbles and 56 green marbles on the ground. What is the mean of marbles of each color?

35. There are number of books in public library. There are 15 Hindi, 25 English, 35 Science, 15 History, and 50 Social Studies books. What is the mean of books of each subject?

36. There are 4 blue pencils, 12 red pencils, 20 yellow pencils, 8 black pencils, and 20 green pencils in a box. What is the value of mode for given number of pencils?

37. Paul has number of fruits in his basket. He has 4 apples, 8 oranges, 12 pineapples, 8 bananas, 8 mangos. What is the average number of fruit of each kind in his basket?

38. There are 4 red marbles, 12 blue marbles, 20 yellow marbles, 8 black marbles, and 6 green marbles on the ground. What is the median value?

39. There are number of books in public library. There are 25 Hindi, 15 English and 35 Social Studies books. What is the median value?

40. There are 8 blue pencils, 12 red pencils, 16 yellow pencils, and 12 purple pencils in a box. What is the average number of pencils of each color in the box?

37. PROBABLE COMBINATIONS

1. Michelle wants to attend one instrument and one language class this summer. She can pick from piano, guitar, jazz or xylophone. She can pick one language Spanish, French or German. How many different combinations of classes can Michelle create?

2. Marty likes to play sports either Tennis or Soccer or Badminton in the morning. He also wants to go either for biking or swimming or jogging in the evening. What different combinations he can choose from in a day?

3. Rishi's mom asked him to buy a fruit and a vegetable from a grocery shop. He can a fruit Apple, Banana, Grapes or Orange. He can choose a vegetable from Potato, Spinach, Okra or Reddish. How many choices he has to buy one fruit and one vegetable?

4. Mr. Dough wants to make a painting. He can choose either a canvas or wooden plank as a base. He can choose either red or green color. How many different kind of combinations can he can choose from?

5. How many combinations can you make with 5 different colored marbles and 3 different colored sticks.

6. John went to an amusement park on his summer vacations. There was different ride at the park roller coaster, boat ride, balloon ride, airplane ride. There were various lunch options there such as burger, sandwich, rice and wrap. John has to choose one ride and one lunch for free as a promotion. How many options are available for him to choose for free promotion?

7. Geeta is picking out his clothes for her party. She can wear a red, green or black top. For pants, she can have jeans, khakis or fleece. How many different combinations can she pick for her dress?

8.   A car dealer has 4 different cars Toyota, Honda, Hyundai, Ford. Each car is available in red, green, white and black colors. If Raman wants to buy one car. How many combinations he can choose from?

9.   Matteo is ordering a cake on his birthday. He has various choices to order from. He can choose either Spiderman, Superman, Blackman or Bagman theme. He also has to choose egg or eggless cake. How many different combinations does Matteo has to choose from?

10.   Pawan drove to San Jose. He had various choices for his lunch and dinner. He can go to Chinese, Indian, Korean, Malaysian, or Mexican restaurants. If he has to spend whole day, there. How many combinations he has for his lunch and dinner?

11.   There are 4 colored bed sheets at my home. There are 4 different colored pillows at my home. How many different combinations of bedding sets can I create?

12.   Rishi likes to read various books and write articles. He wanted to choose from either English or Science or History for reading. He also wanted to do writing exercise in one these subjects. How many combinations he has to do one reading and one writing exercise?

13.   Mathew decided to go on vacations. He can go to Las Angeles by Car, Bus or Airplane. He can stay either at 3-Star or 4-Star hotel. He has to choose one transportation and one hotel. How many combinations he has to choose from?

14.   Ream went to a pizza shop. She has to choose either thin or thick crust. She can select one topping from onion, tomato, pineapple, pepperoni, or sausage. How many different combinations can she create to make her own pizza?

15.   Angelina wants to buy a ring at Jewelry shop. She can have either of these metals gold, silver, or platinum. She can add a diamond, topaz, pearl, ruby or sapphire stone on her ring to make it beautiful. How many different kind of rings she can choose from?

16.   There are 4 different kind of roses (red, white, yellow and pink) in the backyard. There are 3 different kind of tulip (white, yellow and purple). Justin wanted to plug 1 rose and 1 tulip. What different kind of combination he can choose from?

17.   Mike had 3 different colored pencils, and 4 different colored erasers. How many combinations he can take to his school if he has to choose 1 pencil and 1 eraser.

18.   There are 5 different kind of stones and 4 different kind of metals at a jewelry shop. How many different combinations of jewelry can you make using one stone and one metal?

19.   Nick has number of options for his breakfast. He can order pancake, sandwich, omelet or oatmeal. He can have either coffee or tea. How many options he has for his breakfast if has to order one main dish and one drink?

20.   ABC's team coach was selecting a dress code for his team. He had a choice to choose either red or black uniform. He also had a choice to choose shoe's color from black, brown, or red. How many different combinations can he have for his team's dress code?

21.   Sera is picking out a new bike. The bike can be black or blue, and the wheels can be 18 inches, 20 inches or 22 inches of size. How many different combinations does Sera has to choose from?

22.   Matt can choose a language from German, French, Spanish and Hindi in his 3rd grade. He also needs to pick up either computer or science class. How many combinations of classes can he choose from?

23.   There are different colored notebooks and pens available at a bookstore. I can choose red, yellow or black notebook. I can also choose a black, red, brown or white pen. How many combinations can I choose a notebook and a pen?

24.   Mr. Bred went to a furniture a store to buy one chair and one table for his son's room. He saw classic, modern, and arctic tables at the store. Shopkeeper also showed him red light, red heavy, blue light and blue heavy chairs. How many different table and chair sets he can make to choose one table and one chair?

25.   Raman's mom wanted to make a sandwich for him. She has 3 different kind of breads. She also has 5 different kind of vegetables onion, tomato, cabbage, mushroom and spinach. How many different kinds of sandwiches she can make if she has to choose one bread and one vegetable?

26.   Kiran is ordering a combo meal for lunch at a restaurant. She can order sandwich, wrap, Panini or salad. She can order a beverage from soda, lemonade, water or Juice. How many different combinations she can order from?

27.   Rick went to 3 different stores in a mall. First store had red and yellow shirts. Second store had green and purple shirts. Third store had pink and black shirts. He wanted to buy one shirt from each store. How many combinations he could choose from?

28.   Raman has red, green and blue T-shirts. He also has black and brown pants. How many different combinations he can wear?

29.   Lucas went out for a dinner yesterday. There were 5 items in appetizer and 6 items in main dishes at the restaurant. He wanted to choose 1 appetizer and 1 dish. How many different combinations he can choose from?

30. Angelina likes to make web-sites. She has 4 themes in her mind - kite, cloud, lake, and lightning. She has 5 different color in her mind - black, blue, red, yellow and green. She wants to choose one theme and one color to make a perfect web-site. How many combinations she has to choose from?

38.   PROBABILITY PROBLEMS

1.   There are 4 balls on the ground. All 4 balls are purple. If you pick up a ball without looking, how likely is it that you will pick a yellow one?
a) Impossible   b) Certain   c) Probable   d) Unlikely

2.   There are 12 cupcakes on the table. If you pick up a cupcake without looking, how likely is it that you will pick a vanilla one?
a) Impossible   b) Certain   c) Probable   d) Unlikely

3.   There are 20 white shirts in a shop. If you pick up a shirt without looking, how likely is it that you will pick a black one?
a) Impossible   b) Certain   c) Probable   d) Unlikely

4.   There are 14 blue pencils and 7 black pencils in a box. If you pick up a pencil without looking, how likely is it that you will pick a black one?
a) Impossible   b) Certain   c) Probable   d) Unlikely

5.   There are 20 white shirts and 10 black shirts in a shop. If you pick up a shirt without looking, how likely is it that you will pick a black one?
a) Impossible   b) Certain   c) Probable   d) Unlikely

6.   There are 10 bottles of orange juice in a refrigerator. How likely is it that you will pick orange juice without looking?
a) Impossible   b) Certain   c) Probable   d) Unlikely

7.   There are 4 balls on the ground. 3 of them are purple and 1 of them is yellow. If you pick up a ball without looking, how likely is it that you will pick a yellow one?
a) Impossible   b) Certain   c) Probable   d) Unlikely

8. There are 4 balls on the ground. 3 of them are purple and 1 of them is yellow. If you pick up a ball without looking, how likely is it that you will pick a purple one?

a) Impossible   b) Certain   c) Probable   d) Unlikely

9. There are 12 glasses of milkshake and 8 glasses of mango shake on the breakfast table. How likely is it that you will pick up mango shake?

a) Impossible   b) Certain   c) Probable   d) Unlikely

10. There are 12 cupcakes on the table. 8 of them are chocolate cupcakes and rest of them are vanilla cupcakes. If you pick up a cupcake without looking, how likely is it that you will pick a chocolate one?

a) Impossible   b) Certain   c) Probable   d) Unlikely

11. There are 10 bottles of orange juice and 4 bottles of apple juice in the refrigerator. How likely is it that you will pick orange juice without looking?

a) Impossible   b) Certain   c) Probable   d) Unlikely

12. There are 8 red marbles. How likely is it that you will pick a blue one?

a) Impossible   b) Certain   c) Probable   d) Unlikely

13. There are 12 fruits in a basket. 8 of them are apples and 4 of them are oranges? How likely is it that you will pick an orange?

a) Impossible   b) Certain   c) Probable   d) Unlikely

14. There are 14 blue pencils in a box. If you pick up a pencil without looking, how likely is it that you will pick a blue one?

a) Impossible   b) Certain   c) Probable   d) Unlikely

15. There are 12 glasses of milkshake and 8 glasses of mango shake on the breakfast table. How likely is it that you will pick up milkshake?

a) Impossible   b) Certain   c) Probable   d) Unlikely

16. David's mom made 10 cups of tomato soups and 4 cups of chicken soup. How likely is it that you will pick a tomato soup?
a) Impossible   b) Certain   c) Probable   d) Unlikely

17. There are 10 bottles of orange juice and 4 bottles of apple juice in a refrigerator. How likely is it that you will pick apple juice without looking?
a) Impossible   b) Certain   c) Probable   d) Unlikely

18. There are 12 glasses of milkshake on the breakfast table. How likely is it that you will pick up a milkshake?
a) Impossible   b) Certain   c) Probable   d) Unlikely

19. There are 15 video CDs in a cabinet. If you pick up a CD without looking, how likely is it that you will pick a video CD?
a) Impossible   b) Certain   c) Probable   d) Unlikely

20. There are 8 marbles. 6 of them are red and 2 of them are blue. How likely is it that you will pick a red one?
a) Impossible   b) Certain   c) Probable   d) Unlikely

21. There are 10 audio CDs and 15 video CDs in a cabinet. If you pick up a CD without looking, how likely is it that you will pick a video CD?
a) Impossible   b) Certain   c) Probable   d) Unlikely

22. There are 8 marbles. 6 of them are red and 2 of them are blue. How likely is it that you will pick a blue one?
a) Impossible   b) Certain   c) Probable   d) Unlikely

23. There are 12 cupcakes on the table. 8 of them are chocolate cupcakes and rest of them are vanilla cupcakes. If you pick up a cupcake without looking, how likely is it that you will pick a vanilla one?
a) Impossible   b) Certain   c) Probable   d) Unlikely

24.   David's mom made 10 cups of tomato soups and 4 cups of chicken soup. How likely is it that you will pick a chicken soup?
a) Impossible   b) Certain   c) Probable   d) Unlikely

25.   There are 10 audio CDs and 15 video CDs in a cabinet. If you pick up a CD without looking, how likely is it that you will pick an audio CD?
a) Impossible   b) Certain   c) Probable   d) Unlikely

26.   There are 12 fruits in a basket. 12 of them are apples? How likely is it that you will pick an apple?
a) Impossible   b) Certain   c) Probable   d) Unlikely

27.   There are 20 white shirts and 10 black shirts in a shop. If you pick up a shirt without looking, how likely is it that you will pick a white one?
a) Impossible   b) Certain   c) Probable   d) Unlikely

28.   There are 12 fruits in a basket. 8 of them are apples and 4 of them are oranges? How likely is it that you will pick an apple?
a) Impossible   b) Certain   c) Probable   d) Unlikely

29.   David's mom made 10 cups of tomato soups. How likely is it that you will pick a chicken soup?
a) Impossible   b) Certain   c) Probable   d) Unlikely

30.   There are 14 blue pencils and 7 black pencils in a box. If you pick up a pencil without looking, how likely is it that you will pick a blue one?
a) Impossible   b) Certain   c) Probable   d) Unlikely

39.   PROBABILITY AND PROBABLE COMBINATIONS (TRUE OR FALSE)

1.   A car dealer has 4 different cars Toyota, Honda, Hyundai, Ford. Each car is available in red, green, white and black colors. If Raman wants to buy one car. He has 12 choices for his ne x t car.
a) True   b) False

2.   There are 10 bottles of orange juice and 4 bottles of apple juice in a refrigerator. It is likely that you will pick apple juice without looking.
a) True   b) False

3.   There are 12 glasses of milkshake and 8 glasses of mango shake on the breakfast table. It is likely that you will pick up mango shake.
a) True   b) False

4.   There are 14 blue pencils and 7 black pencils in a box. If you pick up a pencil without looking, it is unlikely that you will pick a blue one.
a) True   b) False

5.   David's mom made 10 cups of tomato soups and 4 cups of chicken soup. It is likely that you will pick a tomato soup.
a) True   b) False

6.   There are different colored notebooks and pens available at a bookstore. I can choose red, yellow or black notebook. I can also choose a black, red, brown or white pen. There are only 15 combinations possible to choose 1 notebook and 1 pen.
a) True   b) False

7.   There are 12 glasses of milkshake on the breakfast table. It is impossible that you will pick up a milkshake.
a) True   b) False

8.   There are 14 blue pencils and 7 black pencils in a box. If you pick up a pencil without looking, it is likely that you will pick a black one.

a) True   b) False

9.   Mathew decided to go on vacations. He can go to Las Angeles by Car, Bus or Airplane. He can stay either at 3-Star or 4-Star hotel. He has to choose one transportation and one hotel. He can choose from 6 combinations available to him.
a) True   b) False

10.   There are 12 cupcakes on the table. 8 of them are chocolate cupcakes and rest of them are vanilla cupcakes. If you pick up a cupcake without looking, it is unlikely that you will pick a vanilla one.
a) True   b) False

11.   David's mom made 10 cups of tomato soups and 4 cups of chicken soup. It is unlikely that you will pick a chicken soup.
a) True   b) False

12.   There are 15 video CDs in a cabinet. If you pick up a CD without looking, it is certain that you will pick a video CD.
a) True   b) False

13.   Raman's mom wanted to make a sandwich for him. She has 3 different kind of breads. She also has 5 different kind of vegetables onion, tomato, cabbage, mushroom and spinach. She can make 15 different kinds of sandwiches if she has to choose one bread and one vegetable.
a) True   b) False

14.   There are 20 white shirts and 10 black shirts in a shop. If you pick up a shirt without looking, it is unlikely that you will pick a black one.
a) True   b) False

15.   Lucas went out for a dinner yesterday. There were 5 items in appetizer and 6 item in main dishes at the restaurant. He wanted to choose 1 appetizer and 1 dish. He has 30 different combinations he can choose from.
a) True   b) False

16. Rishi likes to read various books and write articles. He wanted to choose from either English or Science or History for reading. He also wanted to do writing exercise in one these subjects. He has 9 combinations to choose from to do one reading and one writing exercise.
a) True   b) False

17. Raman has red, green and blue T-shirts. He also has black and brown pants. He can wear 6 different combinations.
a) True   b) False

18. There are red 8 marbles. It is impossible that you will pick a blue one.
a) True   b) False

19. There are 4 balls on the ground. All 4 balls are purple. If you pick up a ball without looking, it is impossible that you will pick a yellow one.
a) True   b) False

20. Angelina likes to make web-sites. She has 4 themes in her mind - kite, cloud, lake, and lightning. She has 5 different color in her mind - black, blue, red, yellow and green. She wants to choose one theme and one color to make a perfect web-site. She has 20 choices available to make her web-site.
a) True   b) False

21. There are 14 blue pencils in a box. If you pick up a pencil without looking, it is certain that you will pick a blue one.
a) True   b) False

22. There are 8 marbles. 6 of them are red and 2 of them are blue? It is unlikely that you will pick a blue one?
a) True   b) False

23.   There are 12 fruits in a basket. 8 of them are apples and 4 of them are oranges? It is unlikely that you will pick an apple.
a) True   b) False

24.   Rima went to a pizza shop. She has to choose either thin or thick crust. She can select one topping from onion, tomato, pineapple, pepperoni, or sausage. She has 12 options to make her own pizza.
a) True   b) False

25.   You can make 8 combinations with 5 different colored marbles and 3 different colored sticks.
a) True   b) False

26.   There are 12 glasses of milkshake and 8 glasses of mango shake on the breakfast table. It is unlikely that you will pick up milkshake.
a) True   b) False

27.   Matteo is ordering a cake on his birthday. He has various choices to order from. He can choose either Spiderman, Superman, Blackman or Bagman theme. He also has to choose egg or eggless cake. He has 12 different combinations to choose from.
a) True   b) False

28.   There are 4 balls on the ground. 3 of them are purple and 1 of them is yellow. If you pick up a ball without looking, it is unlikely that you will pick a yellow one.
a) True   b) False

29.   There are 8 marbles. 6 of them are red and 2 of them are blue. It is likely that you will pick a red one.
a) True   b) False

30.   There are 12 fruits in a basket. 12 of them are apples? It is certain that you will pick an apple.
a) True   b) False

31. There are 20 white shirts in a shop. If you pick up a shirt without looking, it is certain that you will pick a black one.
a) True   b) False

32. There are 12 cupcakes on the table. 8 of them are chocolate cupcakes and rest of them are vanilla cupcakes. If you pick up a cupcake without looking, it is likely that you will pick a chocolate one.
a) True   b) False

33. Angelina wants to buy a ring at Jewelry shop. She can have either of these metals gold, silver, or platinum. She can add a diamond, topaz, pearl, ruby or sapphire stone on her ring to make it beautiful. She can create 20 different kind of rings with available choices.
a) True   b) False

34. Rishi's mom asked him to buy a fruit and a vegetable from a grocery shop. He can a fruit Apple, Banana, Grapes or Orange. He can choose a vegetable from Potato, Spinach, Okra or Reddish. She can choose from 20 combinations to buy one fruit and one vegetable.
a) True   b) False

35. Mr. Dough wants to make a painting. He can choose either a canvas or wooden plank as a base. He can choose either red or green color. He has only 2 choices to make his painting with one base and one color.
a) True   b) False

36. There are 10 audio CDs and 15 video CDs in a cabinet. If you pick up a CD without looking, it is unlikely that you will pick a video CD.
a) True   b) False

37. There are 10 audio CDs and 15 video CDs in a cabinet. If you pick up a CD without looking, it is likely that you will pick an audio CD.
a) True   b) False

38. There are 4 different kind of roses (red, white, yellow and pink) in the backyard. There are 3 different kind of tulip (white, yellow and purple). Justin wanted to plug 1 rose and 1 tulip. He can make 12 kind of combinations.
a) True   b) False

39. Rick went to 3 different stores in a mall. First store had red and yellow shirts. Second store had green and purple shirts. Third store had pink and black shirts. He wanted to buy one shirt from each store. He can choose from 6 combinations.
a) True   b) False

40. Pawan drove to San Jose. He had various choices for his lunch and dinner. He can go to Chinese, Indian, Korean, Malaysian, or Mexican restaurants. If he has to spend whole day, there. He has to choose from a maximum of 10 combinations for his lunch and dinner.
a) True   b) False

ANSWERS KEY

1.Divisible Problems (True or False)	2. Greatest Common Factor	3.Least Common Multiple
1. True	1. 5	1. 63
2. False	2. 6	2. 25
3. False	3. 10	3. 2
4. True	4. 2	4. 81
5. False	5. 1	5. 16
6. False	6. 3	6. 72
7. True	7. 3	7. 12
8. True	8. 9	8. 355
9. False	9. 3	9. 28
10. False	10. 7	10. 6
11. True	11. 7	11. 10
12. False	12. 8	12. 14
13. True	13. 1	13. 45
14. False	14. 20	14. 54
15. True	15. 21	15. 4
16. False	16. 18	16. 20
17. False	17. 18	17. 3
18. True	18. 10	18. 45
19. True	19. 2	19. 40
20. False	20. 9	20. 36
21. True	21. 24	21. 6
22. False	22. 2	22. 27
23. False	23. 10	23. 20
24. False	24. 27	24. 30
25. True	25. 12	25. 16
26. True	26. 9	26. 9
27. False	27. 6	27. 50
28. True	28. 30	28. 24
29. False	29. 6	29. 18
30. True	30. 15	30. 8
31. False	31. 6	31. 20
32. True	32. 2	32. 12
33. True	33. 4	33. 18
34. True	34. 7	34. 12
35. True	35. 9	35. 15
36. False	36. 8	36. 21
37. True	37. 4	37. 90
38. True	38. 5	38. 40
39. True	39. 8	39. 36
40. True	40. 6	40. 32

4.Prime or Composite Numbers	39. Composite	6.Square Root of a Number

1. Composite	40. 11 Prime number	1. 5
2. Composite	40. 22 Composite number	2. 41
3. Composite		3. 14
4. Prime	**5.Square of a Number**	4. 32
5. Composite	1. 36	5. 43
6. Prime	2. 1369	6. 44
7. Composite	3. 841	7. 9
8. Composite	4. 1521	8. 3
9. Prime	5. 361	9. 25
10. Prime	6. 1024	10. 17
11. 71 Prime number	7. 729	11. 30
11. 72 Composite number	8. 1764	12. 23
12. Prime	9. 9	13. 36
13. Prime	10. 225	14. 15
14. Prime	11. 121	15. 6
15. Prime	12. 1444	16. 40
16. 97 Prime number	13. 2025	17. 38
16. 27 Composite number	14. 1681	18. 31
17. Prime	15. 25	19. 7
18. Composite	16. 100	20. 33
19. Composite	17. 2304	21. 20
20. Composite	18. 1156	22. 27
21. Composite	19. 676	23. 13
22. Composite	20. 441	24. 11
23. Composite	21. 196	25. 18
24. Composite	22. 900	26. 10
25. Prime	23. 1849	27. 21
26. 83 Prime number	24. 324	28. 22
26. 84 Composite number	25. 961	29. 28
27. Prime	26. 400	30. 4
28. Composite	27. 529	31. 2
29. Composite	28. 1600	32. 16
30. Composite	29. 576	33. 42
31. Prime	30. 1936	34. 39
32. Composite	31. 1225	35. 24
33. Composite	32. 144	36. 8
34. Composite	33. 169	37. 12
35. Prime	34. 2209	38. 19
36. 41 Prime number	35. 625	39. 34
36. 42 Composite number	36. 49	40. 35
37. Composite	37. 2500	
38. 59 Prime number	38. 784	
38. 51 Composite number	39. 2401	
	40. 289	

7.Number Theory (True or False)	8.Determine Ratio	9.Understand Percentage Concept
1. True	1. 10:27	1. 100
2. True	2. 4:1	2. 306
3. True	3. 1:4	3. 4626
4. True	4. 3:4	4. 574
5. True	5. 2:1	5. 2576
6. True	6. 1:20	6. 932
7. True	7. 1:2	7. 1970
8. True	8. 5:9	8. 250
9. False	9. 12:17	9. 636
10. True	10. 5:2	10. 4304
11. True	11. 5:3	11. 650
12. False	12. 1:9	12. 50
13. False	13. 2:5	13. 2220
14. False	14. 15:25	14. 2682
15. True	15. 12:5	15. 1672
16. False	16. 1:5	16. 3934
17. False	17. 1:1	17. 1326
18. True	18. 5:12	18. 3516
19. True	19. 2:3	19. 3050
20. False	20. 3:4	20. 534
21. True	21. 14:20	21. 490
22. True	22. 2:3	22. 464
23. True	23. 5:7	23. 2740
24. False	24. 7:11	24. 226
25. True	25. 1:7	25. 2422
26. False	26. 3:4	26. 616
27. False	27. 4:3	27. 2536
28. True	28. 2:5	28. 404
29. False	29. 5:12	
30. True	30. 7:12	
31. False		
32. True		
33. False		
34. False		
35. True		
36. True		
37. True		
38. False		
39. True		
40. False		

10.Compare and Balance Percentage Values	11.Fraction, Ratio and Percentage (True or False)	12.Fraction, Ratio and Percentage (Word Problems)
1. >	1. False	1. 8:25
2. =	2. False	2. 1 %
3. <	3. False	3. 30 years
4. >	4. True	4. 1:4
5. >	5. False	5. 20
6. <	6. False	6. 1 pound
7. <	7. True	7. 80
8. >	8. True	8. 15:25
9. >	9. False	9. 60
10. >	10. False	10. 4
11. >	11. True	11. 20
12. =	12. False	12. 200
13. >	13. True	13. 1
14. <	14. False	14. 40
15. >	15. True	15. 4:1
16. >	16. True	16. 12:17
17. =	17. True	17. 2
18. >	18. True	18. 3:7
19. <	19. False	19. 20 years
20. >	20. True	20. 1 1/6 (or 7/6)
21. >	21. True	21. 2:1
22. =	22. True	22. 80
23. >	23. True	23. 80
24. =	24. True	24. 75
25. <	25. True	25. 17:8
26. <	26. False	26. 10
27. >	27. True	27. 7:1
28. >	28. True	28. 50
29. >	29. True	29. 2/3
30. <	30. False	30. 1/3
31. >	31. True	31. 1/2
32. <	32. False	32. 25
33. <	33. True	33. 1:2
34. =	34. True	34. 40
35. >	35. True	35. 1:5
36. >	36. False	36. 4/3
37. >	37. True	37. 16
38. =	38. True	38.
39. =	39. False	
40. >	40. False	

13.Relationship between Ratio, Percentage and Fraction	14.Write Mathematical Expressions and Equations	15.Value of Unknown Expression in Mathematical Equations
1. 8/25	1. a/8	1. 21
2. 4:1	2. (n/20) +12	2. 76
3. 1/4	3. 2 x =2	3. -10
4. 25 %	4. a+9	4. 1/2
5. 4:5	5. A x A	5. 2
6. 20 %	6. x +10	6. 5 1/2
7. 10/27	7. n x 10 x 27/2	7. 2
8. 1/4	8. 18/n	8. 22
9. 1:3	9. 97 x m x w	9. 0
10. 50 %	10. t x t x t	10. 7
11. 400 %	11. 5n	11. 10 1/2
12. 70 %	12. A x 10 x 27	12. 1/3
13. 17:8	13. q+8	13. 3/13
14. 2/1	14. 7+n+10	14. 1/3
15. 5/7	15. n+2	15. 2/3
16. 8/25	16. 2 x + 5 = 2	16. 1/5
17. 4/1	17. 14/7	17. 3
18. 1/4	18. 8X10	18. 3
19. 5/2	19. n/2 = 10	19. 8
20. 20 %	20. b x 3	20. 1
21. 17/10	21. n/20 +10	21. 5
22. 50 %	22. 10 - 5	22. 41
23. 17/10	23. 5-s	23. 1
24. 4:5	24. 20n+100	24. 10
25. 10 %	25. (2+n)/3	25. 2
26. 1 %		
27. 25 %		
28. 50 %		
29. 5:12		
30. 1/4		

16.Understand Order of Mathematical Operations and Parentheses	17.Solve Mathematical Equations (True or False)	18.Determine Unit Price of an Object
1. 648	1. False	1. 4
2. -20	2. False	2. 1.2
3. 625	3. False	3. 1.3
4. 0	4. False	4. 50 cents
5. 58	5. True	5. 2
6. 102	6. True	6. 4
7. 9	7. True	7. 2
8. 4	8. False	8. 20
9. 21	9. True	9. 0.50
10. -612	10. True	10. 20
11. 36	11. False	11. 3
12. -10	12. True	12. 1.5
13. 24	13. False	13. 1.1
14. 228	14. True	14. 02.5
15. 67	15. True	15. 0.23
16. 9	16. False	16. 4.5
17. 23	17. True	17. 3
18. 256	18. False	18. 4.17
19. 27	19. True	19. 1.38
20. 140	20. True	20. 28.67
21. 125	21. False	21. Chicago
22. 26	22. False	22. 60 gallons
23. -867	23. True	23. 100 hats pack
24. 18	24. False	24. 10 yards
25. 120	25. True	25. 30 candies for $12
		26. 10 for $45

19.Determine Cost Multiple Objects	20.Convert Length and Height Units	21.Convert Volume Units
1. 2	1. 116 Inches	1. 6 fluid ounces
2. 18	2. 123 Feet	2. 16 quarts
3. 6.5	3. 39 Feet	3. 9 pints
4. 9	4. 41 Inches	4. 56 pints
5. 6	5. 46 Yards 1 Feet	5. 10 pints
6. 80	6. 28 Yards 2 Feet	6. 48 cups
7. 40	7. 1 Feet	7. 4 gallons
8. 120	8. 19 Feet 8 Inches	8. 96 cups
9. 12	9. 254 Inches	9. 1 quart
10. 7.2	10. 5 Feet 6 Inches	10. 12 tablespoons
11. 10	11. 12 Feet 6 Inches	11. 6 cups
12. 6	12. 10 Yards 1 Feet	12. 48 fluid ounces
13. 20	13. 24 Yards 0 Feet	13. 6 tablespoons
14. 3	14. 37 Inches	14. 192 cups
15. 3	15. 9 Feet 2 Inches	15. 4 pints
16. 100	16. 13 Feet 6 Inches	16. 7 gallons
17. 120	17. 12 Feet 0 Inches	17. 1 gallons
18. 16	18. 24 Yards 0 Feet	18. 1 pints
19. 30	19. 200 Inches	19. 18 cups
20. 9	20. 46 Yards 2 Feet	20. 5 quarts
	21. 68 Feet	21. 1 quarts
	22. 101 Inches	22. 64 fluid ounces
	23. 265 Inches	23. 1 pint
	24. 20 Feet 1 Inches	24. 12 quarts
	25. 122 Feet	25. 12 tablespoons

22.Convert Weight Units	23.Measurement Problems (True or False)	24.Measure Length using Metric System
1. 7 Tons 400 lb.	1. False	1. 876.123
2. 3 Tons 800 lb.	2. False	2. 9877.865
3. 86 oz.	3. False	3. 1010
4. 2 lb. 2 oz.	4. True	4. 20.302
5. 18 Tons 0 lb.	5. True	5. 1
6. 4 Tons 1200 lb.	6. True	6. 1500
7. 166 oz.	7. True	7. 9898.89
8. 19,600 lb.	8. True	8. 500
9. 18 Tons 100 lb.	9. False	9. 51.42
10. 14, 800 lb.	10. False	10. 123.45
11. 32 oz.	11. False	11. 1000
12. 4 Tons 200 lb.	12. False	12. 10120
13. 2800 lb.	13. False	13. 98767.8
14. 29 oz.	14. False	14. 2321
15. 14, 300 lb.	15. False	15. 2100
16. 9 Tons 200 lb.	16. True	16. 10
17. 56 oz.	17. False	17. 3100
18. 52 oz.	18. True	18. 876.54
19. 7 Tons 600 lb.	19. True	19. 9.8
20. 4 Tons	20. True	20. 510
21. 3 lb. 2 oz.	21. False	21. 1200
22. 57 oz.	22. False	22. 89.71
23. 73 oz.	23. False	23. 1000
24. 1 lb. 1 oz.	24. False	24. 334.433
25. 9 Tons 0 lb.	25. True	25. 8.176
	26. False	
	27. False	
	28. True	
	29. True	
	30. True	
	31. False	
	32. True	
	33. True	
	34. False	

25. Measure Volume using Metric system	26. Measure Weight using Metric system	27. Measurements using Metric System (True or False)
1. 42.42	1. 60620	1. True
2. 2020	2. 787.887	2. True
3. 7377.364	3. 500	3. True
4. 2000	4. 87.654	4. True
5. 2200	5. 5.642	5. True
6. 3200	6. 20.502	6. True
7. 20220	7. 6000	7. True
8. 20.302	8. 554.455	8. True
9. 2	9. 6000	9. True
10. 376.44	10. 62.545	10. True
11. 223.44	11. 8.776	11. True
12. 7.3	12. 60	12. True
13. 73767.3	13. 7877.865	13. True
14. 2200	14. 6	14. True
15. 420	15. 876.625	15. True
16. 2000	16. 5600	16. True
17. 20	17. 2526	17. True
18. 2322	18. 6500	18. True
19. 37.72	19. 8.676	19. True
20. 400	20. 2600	20. True
21. 2400	21. 560	21. True
22. 376.223	22. 6200	22. True
23. 7373.37	23. 7876.78	23. True
24. 334.433	24. 6060	24. True
25. 3.276	25. 0.78	

28.Conversion of Time Units (Hours, Minutes and Seconds)	29.Conversion of Time using Multiple Time Units	30.Time Problems (True or False)
1. 8	1. 23	1. False
2. 4	2. 31	2. True
3. False	3. 22	3. True
4. 480	4. 498	4. True
5. True	5. 6	5. True
6. 180	6. 4	6. True
7. 7	7. 2	7. False
8. 600	8. 5	8. True
9. 1440	9. 320	9. True
10. 540	10. 3	10. False
11. 60	11. 5	11. False
12. 6	12. 4	12. False
13. 5	13. 8	13. True
14. 5	14. 7	14. True
15. False	15. 377	15. True
16. True	16. 30	16. True
17. 360	17. 315	17. False
18. 5	18. 30	18. False
19. True	19. 6	19. True
20. 300	20. 6	20. True
21. False	21. 2	21. False
22. 60	22. 5	22. True
23. 480	23. 74	23. True
24. 24	24. 12	24. False
25. 120	25. 2	25. False
26. 6	26. 5	26. True
27. 360	27. 2	27. True
28. 4	28. 12	28. True
29. 7	29. 15	29. False
30. 300	30. 2	30. False
31. 240	31. 3	31. True
32. 420	32. 7	32. False
	33. 122	33. False
	34. 15	34. False
	35. 36	35. False
	36. 99	36. True
	37. 214	37. True
	38. 255	38. False
	39. 275	39. False
	40. 630	40. True

31.Understand Time Schedule	32.Time Word Problems (Elapsed Time, Start Time and End Time)	33.Average, Mean, Median
1. 1 H :15 M	1. 4:40	1. 20
2. 6 Minutes	2. 8:45	2. 22
3. 15 Minutes	3. 1:25	3. 17
4. 10:40:00 AM	4. 1:00	4. 8
5. Fish Feeding	5. 10:00	5. 10
6. 45 Minutes	6. 2:25	6. 16
7. 5 Minutes	7. 11:00	7. 11
8. Schools tour with the principal	8. 1:45	8. 10
9. Science	9. 2:45	9. 12
10. 15 Minutes	10. 7:45	10. 20
11. Lunch Break	11. 6:45	11. 10
12. 11:55:00 AM	12. 1:05	12. 16
13. 11:50:00 AM	13. 2:30	13. 10
14. Students induction	14. 4:15	14. 27
15. 6 Minutes	15. 2:00	15. 6
16. Monkey Show	16. 1:20	16. 12
17. 10:35:00 AM	17. 1:30	17. 12
18. 30 Minutes	18. 6:15	18. 11
19. 12 Minutes	19. 8:00	19. 12
20. 30 Minutes	20. 11:10	20. 14
		21. 6
		22. 21
		23. 12
		24. 12
		25. 6
		26. 14
		27. 15
		28. 10
		29. 16
		30. 21
		31. 17
		32. 40
		33. 6
		34. 15
		35. 8
		36. 14
		37. 25
		38. 22
		39. 6
		40. 11

34.Mode and Range	35.Average, Mean, Median, Mode and Range (True or False)	36.Average, Mean, Median, Mode and Range (word problems)
1. 7	1. False	1. 6
2. 24	2. True	2. 22
3. 10	3. True	3. 18
4. 27	4. True	4. 6
5. 30	5. False	5. 22
6. 9	6. False	6. 4
7. 20	7. True	7. 16
8. 40	8. False	8. 6
9. 16	9. False	9. 16
10. 6	10. True	10. 8
11. 66	11. False	11. 22
12. 3	12. False	12. 18
13. 18	13. False	13. 18
14. 32	14. False	14. 12
15. 22	15. True	15. 22
16. 16	16. True	16. 18
17. 25	17. False	17. 10
18. 25	18. True	18. 6
19. 30	19. False	19. 9
20. 33	20. True	20. 4
21. 26	21. False	21. 20
22. 28	22. True	22. 30
23. 52	23. True	23. 26
24. 34	24. False	24. 25
25. 20	25. False	25. 6
26. 16	26. False	26. 11
27. 30	27. True	27. 6
28. 9	28. False	28. 28
29. 30	29. True	29. 9
30. 35	30. False	30. 18
31. 12	31. True	31. 8
32. 33	32. False	32. 18
33. 12	33. True	33. 11
34. 12	34. False	34. 18
35. 12	35. True	35. 28
36. 27	36. False	36. 20
37. 22	37. False	37. 8
38. 30	38. False	38. 8
39. 24	39. True	39. 25
40. 6	40. False	40. 12

37.Probable Combinations	38.Probability Problems	39.Probability and Probable Combinations (True or False)
1. 12	1. Impossible	1. True
2. 9	2. Impossible	2. False
3. 16	3. Impossible	3. False
4. 4	4. Unlikely	4. False
5. 15	5. Unlikely	5. True
6. 16	6. Certain	6. False
7. 9	7. Unlikely	7. False
8. 12	8. Probable	8. False
9. 8	9. Unlikely	9. True
10. 25	10. Probable	10. True
11. 16	11. Probable	11. True
12. 9	12. Impossible	12. True
13. 6	13. Unlikely	13. True
14. 10	14. Certain	14. True
15. 15	15. Probable	15. True
16. 12	16. Probable	16. True
17. 12	17. Unlikely	17. True
18. 20	18. Certain	18. True
19. 8	19. Certain	19. True
20. 6	20. Probable	20. True
21. 6	21. Probable	21. True
22. 8	22. Unlikely	22. True
23. 12	23. Unlikely	23. False
24. 12	24. Unlikely	24. False
25. 15	25. Unlikely	25. False
26. 16	26. Certain	26. False
27. 6	27. Probable	27. False
28. 6	28. Probable	28. True
29. 30	29. Impossible	29. True
30. 20	30. Probable	30. True
		31. False
		32. True
		33. False
		34. False
		35. False
		36. False
		37. False
		38. True
		39. True
		40. False

101Minute.com

Welcome to 101Minute.com, a guide dedicated to help students excel academically.

We are focused on creating educational programs that help to enhance student's skills across various grades and subjects. Modules are designed per grade level that progressively enhances their skill and confidence each day.

Each subject category has several quizzes designed to assess student's mastery with the concept. By consistently devoting 101 minutes per week, students can demonstrate significant improvement.

We are committed to serving our student community by building effective tools and reward programs. We are open to receiving feedback on how we can improve to make this an even better experience for our students. Our goal is to create a fun and learning social educational environment for students, and reward them for their achievements.

Please visit us at 101Minute.com.

Practice 101 Minutes Weekly to Master Your Math Skills

Made in the USA
Middletown, DE
27 May 2020

96073052R00077